RING THE BELL AND COUNT THE PEOPLE
And Other Stories from the Village

By Harold P. Kurtz
Author of *Hardly a Silent Night*

Kirk House Publishers
Minneapolis, Minnesota

Ring the Bell and Count the People
And Other Stories from the Village
By Harold P. Kurtz
Copyright 2008 Harold Kurtz. All rights reserved.

ISBN 13: 978-1-933794-12-9
ISBN 10: 1-933794-12-7

LCCN: 2008935314

Kirk House Publishers, PO Box 390759, Minneapolis, Minnesota
Manufactured in the United Sates of America

TABLE OF CONTENTS

Mother Writes a Disclaimer 5

Those Cute Little Shelves 8

Why There Was No Sunday Sermon 21

Dad and the Singing Hollanders 33

The Mystery at the Gas Station 42

Cousin George Decides to Leave Town 53

Helene Learns to Eat a Cream Puff 65

What Was in Mr. Schiffler's Barn 80

Cousin Esther and the Poor Little Piggies 90

The Greatest Village Event Ever 99

The Halloween Hunt Goes Askew 113

What Happened to the Huehne Kids 123

Ring the Bell and Count the People 135

The Year Comes to an End 143

Appreciation 146

About the Author 148

DEDICATION

To Emily and Joshua
who like stories

MOTHER WRITES A DISCLAIMER

First, about our family. There were five of us: my mother, my father, my older brother, Philip, my younger sister, Helene, and me. (If you've read my first book, *Hardly a Silent Night*, you can just skip over this part. But if you haven't read it, or maybe you've forgotten some of the details, then keep on reading.)

About the time World War II started, we moved from Milwaukee, Wisconsin, to the Village, a small town in eastern Wisconsin. Dad was the pastor of Emanuel Lutheran Church in the Village, and we lived in the parsonage, right next to the church building. When I wrote *Hardly a Silent Night*, it was mainly about what happened at Christmas time a while back. Since the Village was a small town, we knew everyone, and everyone certainly knew us. Preachers' families tend to be in the public eye.

Anyway, World War II had been over for a few years, and life had returned to normal for most people. For some families, life would never be the same since they had a son or brother or other family member who had been killed in the war.

Inside Emanuel, the Honor Roll still hung on the side wall. It listed all the members of the congregation who had served in the War, and beside two of the names were stars, indicating they had died in the War.

But for most people, life was back to normal. Food and gas rationing were over. This meant we could buy sugar and make Kool Aid at home. When we had a nickel, we could buy a Hershey or a Milky Way candy bar which were rarely available during the War.

Dad had even gotten a new car—a shiny gray four-door Chevrolet Stylemaster, which replaced the 1934 two-door Chevy he had driven all those years.

So here are some stories about life in the Village.

Now, I won't go so far as to say they're totally true. Some of them may have happened, but you should know that here and there I may have stretched the truth a bit and have added a few details which may not have exactly taken place, and I changed some of the people too. But if you think that everything didn't exactly happen the way it takes place in the book, well, it could have been the way I described it, or then again, maybe my memory is better than yours.

Before I go further I better explain a few things about our family and about my earlier book, *Hardly a Silent Night*. I hadn't really planned to write another book after *Hardly a Silent Night*. Writing is tough work, and I certainly have enough other things to do with my time.

But a lot of things have happened since last Christmas, plus I've remembered other things worth telling, so that's why you're reading a new book.

The family had varied reactions to the idea of a new book. My sister said there should be more things about her, since after all, she said a lot of cute things, and I wouldn't even have to make them up like I did last time. Phil said he would be just as happy if I left him out of the book entirely. Dad just smiled and said something to the effect that if I wanted to write, I should go ahead and do it. Besides, he liked the way I talked about some of the members of the congregation.

As for Mother's reaction, she complained that I exaggerated things.

"If you're going to write another book about us, I think I should have a chance to set the record straight," she intoned.

"What do you mean—'set the record straight?'" I asked.

"Well..." Mother hesitated and then continued, "you know, so the members won't get upset."

Oh, the members. Mother was always worried about what the members of Emanuel might say about her or her children. (She never was concerned about what they thought about Dad. Since he was the pastor, it seemed to me that this should be her chief concern. But no, it was always what the members might think about her or her children.)

I learned long ago that it was best not to argue with Mother since I never could win an argument with her. So I told Mother that if she wanted to have her say, she could write her own introduction to the book. This is what she wrote.

Mother's Disclaimer

Before you read this book, I feel there are some things you better understand. I am the author's mother, and I'm proud to have a son who writes books. I haven't had a chance to read this book yet—he said I could read it when it was published.

If it's like his earlier book, *Hardly a Silent Night*, you'll enjoy it. But it's only fair to warn you that not everything he writes is true. Oh sure, most of the things are correct. After all, it wouldn't be right to say that he lied about things. My son wouldn't do that, especially since he's the pastor's son.

But there are some things he writes about that are not quite as I remember them, especially when he's writing about me. As he always tells the family, he never let the facts interfere with a good story.

So I think it's only fair to warn you that you shouldn't believe everything he writes, even though it sounds good. Now if you remember *Hardly a Silent Night*, he said that I wanted the family to be a famous performing group. I never said that (well, maybe once); I just thought it would be a nice thing if the family could be together and sing and play some of the songs which we do in our living room at Christmas time.

And he claimed that I was always scared my children would come down with pneumonia and that I made them wear so many clothes in winter. Well, that may be true, but if they get sick, you know who has to take care of them. He needs to listen to his mother.

I could go on and on (author's note: she usually does) but I won't—this time. All I want you to know is not to believe everything he writes about me. If he isn't careful, I may have to write my own book.

The Author's Mother

THOSE CUTE LITTLE SHELVES

Bobby Draeger was one of my best friends, but one summer he certainly caused me a major problem. It really wasn't his fault. It was Mother who was the source of trouble. Bobby was an innocent bystander.

I guess I had better explain things. Bobby's dad was the Lutheran pastor in Rosendale, a neighboring town to the Village. Pastor Draeger and his wife were good friends of my parents. Our family and the Draegers would often visit each other.

That's how Bobby and I got to be friends. We would be together when our families visited. Sometimes he would come and stay with me for a few days, or I would visit him, doing various things together with his friend Don. One summer the three of us were in the same cabin at Bible Camp.

Once when our family was visiting the Draegers, Mother noticed that Mrs. Draeger had some new little shelves in her kitchen. Mother admired them and asked Mrs. Draeger where she had gotten them.

"Oh," said Mrs. Draeger, "Bobby made them."

Mother was astonished. "Bobby made them? They really are nice."

Mother was Norwegian, and I always felt there was something genetic about Norwegians and how they admired people who worked with wood. Mother's father was an excellent carpenter, and many of her family were skilled woodworkers.

Mother didn't feel that Dad would ever do much in woodworking. After all, he was German, and Mother felt that Germans weren't as good as Norwegians when it came to woodworking. However, Mother did feel that given the right circumstances, one of her sons could probably become an accomplished woodworker. They were half Norwegian, she reasoned.

Mrs. Draeger explained that Bobby had saved his money and had purchased a small jig saw from Sears Roebuck.

"He didn't even need a pattern for the shelves," Mrs. Draeger told Mother. "He just figured it out."

As we drove back to the Village from our visit, Mother told us all about how Bobby had made these cute shelves with his new saw.

"And he's not even Norwegian," she exclaimed.

I didn't pay much attention. If Bobby wanted to make shelves for his mother, good for him, I thought. It wasn't anything which interested me.

A few days later at the supper table, Mother brought up the subject of the shelves.

"You know," she said to me, "I bet you could make some nice things if you just had a saw like Bobby's."

I pointed out that I didn't have a saw, I didn't have any money to buy one, and in addition, I wasn't interested. I tried to change the subject.

"Besides, if you want some shelves, have Grandpa Olson make them for you," I told her.

Grandpa Olson was Mother's dad. He was a good carpenter. He made a lot of things for us.

"Well," Mother replied, "I don't know if he will be coming to visit us. Besides, he would need that type of saw to make the shelves."

Mother dropped the subject. However, a couple of weeks later she brought up the saw again.

"We just got the new Sears Roebuck catalog," she announced. "The saw like Bobby Draeger has is on sale."

"How do you know what kind of saw he has?" I asked.

"Mrs. Draeger showed it to me," Mother answered. "He paid $29.95 for his, and now it's on sale for $19.95."

I did not like the way the conversation was heading. I thought back to a year or so ago when Mother had coerced Phil into buying an accordion. It cost Phil many weeks of pay from his job at the filling station, and now the accordion just sat in the closet.

Usually I could get Mother distracted by picking a fight with my brother, but he wasn't home for supper this evening; he was off working at his job.

"But I don't have $19.95 plus there's the mailing cost too," I protested.

Mother paused. She knew I didn't have the money. I made a little money mowing lawns during the summer, but that wasn't very much. I got fifty cents for one lawn and seventy five cents for the other one.

"And even if I didn't spend anything, it would take four months to save that much and lawns won't need mowing that long," I pointed out to Mother.

Mother thought for a moment.

"Don't forget the money you make selling night crawlers," she countered.

She was right. The highway through the Village led to a number of good fishing lakes. I had developed a little business selling night crawlers—the large worms which came out at night after rains. Fishermen liked to use them for bait.

"But I only get twenty-five cents a dozen, and I never know if I will sell any or not, and if it gets dry, there won't be any to sell," I told her.

Supper was over. We had our devotions. My sister and I cleared the table and helped with the dishes. Mother dropped the subject.

I was worried. I knew how persistent Mother was. I thought back to how she got Phil to buy an accordion. He took lessons, but he soon lost interest, and the accordion sat in the closet except when Dad played it.

Dad could do a lot of things, I thought. I remembered the time he had done a painting of the Silent Night Christmas carol, and we had won the prize in the decorating contest. Or the time he had surprised Mother by making a pottery vase.

A few days later Mother brought up the subject again while we were having supper.

"You know," she said, "that sale only runs for three weeks more. It sure would be great if you could get that saw and make some nice little shelves."

"Even if I did have the money for the saw, I would need money for wood for the shelves," I told her.

"No, you wouldn't." Phil interjected. "We have all the wooden boxes."

I glared at Phil. He was no help at all. He was right: we did have all those wooden boxes which could be taken apart and used for wood. We had gotten a whole truckload of wooden packing boxes when Cousin George was working at the canning factory in the Village.

Getting back to the discussion with Mother.

"Yes," replied Mother, "there is plenty of wood. You could make all sorts of shelves and other things if you had that nice saw."

"But where would I get $20?" I asked. "Besides, there's the cost of postage too."

"Well, if you order it, we'll pay the shipping," Mother promised.

"OK," I said, "if by some miracle I can come up with $20 before the sale ends, I'll buy the saw."

I figured I was safe. There was no way I would come up with $20 in the next two weeks. It had been real dry for the past several weeks which meant that the lawns I usually mowed weren't growing, and it also meant that there were no night crawlers to hunt since they only came out after it rained. Besides, once the sale ended, maybe Mother would forget about the shelves and the saw.

Wouldn't you know. The next day it started to rain, and it rained all day, all night and the next morning. By noon it had stopped, and the weather began to clear.

I was looking out the window when I saw a pickup truck pull into the driveway. I didn't recognize the truck.

A man got out of the truck and came to the door. I opened the door, and the man said,

"I saw your sign on the highway. Got any night crawlers?"

"No," I answered, "it's been too dry. But I'll have some tomorrow."

"My name is Bud Norton. I have a guide service at Green Lake. I have a big group coming from Chicago this weekend. I'm out of bait and my regular supplier can't help me. I'm going to be coming back this way about 12 tonight. Do you think you could have 1,000 night crawlers by then?"

A thousand night crawlers, I thought. Most people only bought a dozen or two.

"If you can," he continued, "I'll give you $20."

Twenty dollars! That's about as much as I make in the whole summer mowing lawns.

I was so stunned by the offer that I said, "Yes, I think I can have that many night crawlers by midnight" and forgot that I had promised Mother I would order the saw if somehow I would get $20.

"OK," replied Bud, "see you about midnight."

I closed the door What had I gotten myself into? How could I ever collect that many night crawlers in one evening.

Then it hit me. If I did get that many night crawlers I would have to buy the saw. But if I didn't try. . . well, I had given my word to the man, so I had to do my best.

Mother was talking to Dad in his study I interrupted them as I walked in.

"I've got a big problem," I told them.

I explained the situation.

"We can all help," Mother replied. "Dad and I can go out. Phil isn't working tonight, and I'm sure he will help if I ask him."

That evening we gathered around the kitchen table. I outlined how we would do things.

"Mother and Helene can stay around here. You can make a circuit of the gardens in our block and the next. Then repeat the route about every 15-20 minutes," I said.

I had permission from the neighbors to hunt night crawlers in their gardens. All they asked is that I go along the edges and not step on any plants.

"Phil, why don't you take the athletic field. That's usually a good place to hunt," I continued. "And, Dad, maybe you could do the park. I'll get the lawns and gardens on the other side of the church. When your cans get full, bring them back and dump them in the containers in back."

Catching night crawlers is not all that easy. You had to bend over and be quick. Although they supposedly couldn't see the light from your flashlight, they could sense when someone was near. They would come out at night to dry off after a rain but would lie with their tail in the hole. You had to make a quick grab at the tail end and be careful not to pull too hard or it would break.

So off we went. Since it didn't get dark in the summer until late, we did not have a long time to hunt. But with four of us—five if you counted my sister—we should be able to do it, I thought.

Mother and Helene quit early since it was past Helene's bedtime. Dad, Phil and I kept working. It was about 11:30 when we headed home.

What an amazing sight—the large, stone crocks where I kept the night crawlers looked like a scene from a jungle film. Now I had a real job—counting them.

Around midnight I triumphantly announced, "We did it. There are 1,020 of them."

Dad, Phil and I went and sat on the front steps, waiting for Bud to appear. It was soon 12:15. No sign of him.

"What if he doesn't come?" Phil asked.

"I'm sure he will. He gave me his name and what he did," I replied. But, I thought, what if he didn't come. What would I do with all those night crawlers? That was more t than I sold the entire summer.

Twelve thirty came.

Phil yawned and said "I think I'll go to bed."

Dad and I continued to sit on the steps.

Fifteen minutes went by. I began to worry.

"What if he doesn't come?" I asked Dad.

Before he could answer, we saw headlights and the truck pulled up in front of the house. There was Bud.

"Sorry I'm late. I had a flat tire. How did you do?" he asked.

"We have 1,020 of them for you," I replied.

"Great. I'll get my bait container from the truck."

We went to the back of the house where he filled the container and then carried it to the truck.

"Here's your $20," he said, handing me two ten dollar bills. "And thanks for your hard work. I may need to contact you again."

"Thank you," I told him. "I had a lot of help from my family."

Those Cute Little Shelves • 13

Bud smiled and got into his truck. He waved as he pulled away.

"Well," Dad said, "I think it's bedtime. It's been quite a night."

I slept late the next morning. When I got up, I checked my billfold—the $20 was still there. It was the most money I had ever had.

Then I remembered. I had promised Mother I would buy the saw.

Darn, I thought. Why in the world had I ever promised to do that? I never in the world thought I would earn $20.

But I had given my word. Well, maybe it would be neat to have that saw. I might be able to do all sorts of things with it.

So we ordered the saw and in due course when I stopped at the post office to get our mail, there was a red parcel slip in our box.

I went to the window and handed the slip to Cap Regel, the postmaster.

"This is pretty heavy," he said. "Think you can manage it, or should you have your dad come with the car?"

"I think I can handle it," I answered. "It's not that far."

It was only two and a half blocks home, but I had to stop and rest several times, especially walking up the hill.

"Well, it came," I announced as I entered the kitchen. Mother and Helene gathered around as I placed the box on the table.

I opened the box and there it stood: a Sears Roebuck Craftsman Magnetic Jig Saw.

As I read the instructions, I found that it was not like the jig saw Uncle Alfred had where the blade moved up and down, cutting the wood. This saw had a motor which made the blade vibrate. The vibrations caused the saw to cut the wood.

"It doesn't look too difficult," I said, as I finished reading the instructions.

"You be careful. Don't go cutting your fingers off," Mother warned.

Now she tells me, I thought. Whose idea was this anyway?

I took the saw out to the barn. I got the hammer and dismantled several wooden boxes. I started practicing on some of the smaller boards. It was hard cutting in a straight line. I ruined a lot of boards trying to get some straight cuts. I got some cuts which were fairly straight, but when I tried nailing them together, the wood split. I continued trying, but did not fare any better.

I cleaned the saw, put it back in its box and brought it into the house. Where should I put it? The perfect place, in the closet right next to Phil's accordion.

I reported to Mother that thus far I had been totally unsuccessful in building little shelves for her.

"The next time we visit the Draegers, you can get Bobby to show you how to do things," Mother said encouragingly. I nodded and left the room.

A few nights later at the supper table, a different topic came up.

"Uncle Carl and Aunt Esther would like to get away for a few days," Mother said. They wondered if I would be willing to come and stay with Dad while they and the kids are away."

When Mother said "Dad," she was referring to her father, our Grandfather Olson. Grandpa Olson lived with Mother's brother Carl and his family in a small town in southwestern Wisconsin.

"Can we come too?" Helene asked.

We all enjoyed being with Grandpa Olson. He was always glad to see his grandchildren and liked playing games with them, any kind of games, especially checkers. Phil had noted, however, since he had gotten so he could regularly beat him in checkers, Grandpa was less interested in the game. But he was still willing to play most other games we would suggest.

"If Phil can get off work, I thought he could drive the car there. Do you think you can get some time off?" Mother asked Phil.

"I probably can. Some of the guys who used to work at the station are home from college, and one of them would probably work for a few days. I'll check and see," Phil answered.

Everything went as planned. We had a good time visiting Grandpa Olson and seeing other relatives in Avoca. We had a lot of fun playing games with Grandpa. He and Phil went fishing a couple of times. My Uncle Alfred Olson was a rural mail carrier, and I rode along on his mail route.

Uncle Carl and Aunt Esther and their children returned from their trip. They thanked Mother for coming. We loaded the car and began the drive home.

"I wonder if Dad has done anything special while we were gone," Phil said as we rode along.

"He usually does while we're away," Mother said.

"Remember the time he made the vase?" I asked.

"And when he did the painting?" Phil recalled.

We all nodded. Several other incidents were mentioned.

"Have you noticed that Dad hardly ever does anything more than once?" Phil asked.

"I don't know why that is," Mother answered. "He'll do something. It will turn out fine and then he won't do it again. It always seems he does these things when we're away, and he gets bored."

We continued to ride through the Wisconsin countryside. It was late afternoon when we arrived home.

Dad came out to meet us.

"It's great having you back," he told us. "I was pretty lonely without you."

We unpacked the car and went into the house.

Mother stopped in the kitchen.

"Where did those come from?" she asked.

Dad smiled.

"Where did what come from?" Helene wanted to know.

"There," Mother said, pointing to the counter by the sink. On either side of the sink stood small, white shelves just like the ones Bobby Draeger had made.

"For heaven's sakes, Henry," Mother exclaimed. "Did you make those?"

Dad nodded modestly. "I thought I would try using Harold's saw. I guess I have a little more woodworking talent than I thought."

We all laughed because Dad was not very handy when it came to working with tools.

We crowded round, looking at them.

"Why, Henry, they're wonderful," Mother sad. "They're just what I wanted."

"See," she told me, "I told you that saw would be just the thing for making those little shelves."

I agreed. I figured I was now off the hook and wouldn't have to worry about using the saw any more.

Too bad I had to waste twenty dollars buying it.

A few days later, Mother brought up the subject of the shelves as we were eating supper.

"You know, " she said to me, "now that Dad has made those shelves, you could use them as a pattern and make some more of them. Dad would be glad to help you."

"You've got your shelves. Besides, even if I could build them, what would I do with them?" I responded.

"Why, you could sell them," Mother persisted.

"Where would I sell them?" I wanted to know.

Phil cut in "You could sell them at the tent sale."

"Tent sale? Can we buy one?" Helene asked.

"Buy what?" Dad asked.

"A tent," Helene replied. "It would be a fun to have a tent. We could put it up in the backyard, and my friends and I could play in it. We could even have a sleep over in it."

"It's not a sale of tents," Phil told her. "The merchants in town are going to sponsor a sale in a big tent."

Phil explained that he had heard at work that the business association in the Village was going to sponsor a sale where people could bring items to sell.

"The merchants thought it would be a good way to get people to come to the Village, and then while they are here for the sale, they would probably shop in the stores," Phil said. "There's going to be a section where kids can bring things to sell."

Great, I thought, now Mother will really be after me to make those shelves.

Later that week I picked up information which told about the sale. For fifty cents, kids could have a place at a table where they could sell things. Adults had to pay two dollars.

Then the idea struck me. It would be worth fifty cents, I thought. If it works out, it would be worth a lot more than fifty cents.

After I got paid for mowing Mrs. Grindemann's lawn, I took fifty cents and went down to the store and reserved a place for the sale. I did not tell anyone else what I had done.

Mother had her shelves, and as far as I was concerned, there was no need to keep the saw. I would try to sell it at the tent sale. It was mine, after all.

The day before the tent sale, I took the saw out of the box and carefully cleaned it, removing the sawdust from when Dad had made the shelves. I then got the current Sears Roebuck catalog and cut out the picture, description and price of the saw. I pasted it on a sheet of paper. Then using a black crayon, I carefully printed:

I pasted the sheet on a piece of cardboard and then made an easel out of another piece of cardboard, so it would stand up. I was all set for the sale.

> **HARDLY USED**
>
> CURRENT CATALOG
> PRICE: $29.95
> (plus shipping)
>
> SPECIAL SALE PRICE:
> $25.00

The instructions said that the sale would run from ten in the morning until four in the afternoon and that sellers should be there by 9:30. When I arrived at the tent, a large crowd was milling around, waiting for the sale to start. I showed my reservation slip and was directed to the kids section.

I saw a lot of my friends there, getting set up.

My friend Norm was busy unpacking several boxes of toys.

"Is there space at the table, Norm?" I asked.

"Sure, he replied. "Help yourself."

I unpacked the saw, placed it on the table and set up the easel. I was ready.

"Where did you get all these?" I said to Norm.

"They're my old toys plus some from my sister. Mom said I should see if I can sell them, to get rid of some of the clutter around the house. Where did you get that?" he asked, pointing to my saw.

"Oh, my mother thought it would be a good thing for me to have, so I could make things, but I decided I wasn't all that interested in woodworking," I told him.

I glanced around. Everything you could think of was for sale. Some of the farm kids were selling berries and vegetables. One girl had a big assortment of doll clothes. My friend Arlyn had a display of stamps.

"They're all duplicates, so I thought I would see if I could sell them," he informed me when I stopped by his table.

I was going to look at some of the other tables, when Mr. Crosley, the banker, who was in charge of the sale, made an announcement.

"All right, everyone. I hope you're all set. We're going to let people in now, so everyone should get to their tables. If you have any questions or problems, see me or one of the committee members."

"OK," boomed Mr. Crosley through his microphone, "the sale is now open."

A swarm of people came through the entrance. A steady stream of people came by our table. Many kids stopped at Norm's table, and I could see he was selling a lot of things.

"Mom said the secret is not to price things too high. She said it was better to sell the things than to lug them home and that people are really looking for bargains," he told me during a lull in business.

Hmm, I thought, I wonder if my price is too high. A few people had stopped and looked at my saw, but no one asked about it.

I glanced over at Arlyn's table.

"Any business?" I called to him.

"Sold a few. I don't think there are many stamp collectors here," he answered.

"I think we should be selling toys. Norm seems to be doing pretty well," I told him.

I continued to sit at the table, but no one seemed interested.

"You're not getting any business," Norm said, "Maybe you ought to try something different, like holding a raffle."

"What do you mean, a raffle?" I asked.

"People buy a chance for a big item, but the chance doesn't cost very much. That way they may end up with a big prize for just a little money," Norm explained.

I pondered this information.

"Isn't that gambling?" I wondered.

"No, not really. Our church does it all the time at its festivals," Norm said. "Tell you what. If you watch my table, I'll run home for some lunch and then bring back some blank raffle chances. I know we have a bunch of them left over from the last church festival."

Norm returned, and I walked home for lunch.

I quickly ate a sandwich, got a piece of cardboard, a black crayon, and made a sign. I carried it back to the sale and set it by the saw.

People began stopping by.

"The drawing will be at four o'clock, at the end of the sale. You don't have to be here to win," I told people.

I started selling chances, having people fill out the forms Norm had brought.

"Put your name and phone number on the entry form," I told people. I took one of Norm's empty boxes and put the entry forms into it.

```
WIN
A $29 DOLLAR
JIGSAW


FIFTY CENTS
FOR A CHANCE
```

By 2:30 I had more than 30 entries, and people continued to stop and buy chances. I lost count, but by four o'clock I knew I would come out ahead.

At four o'clock, I announced to those standing around, "Last chance." I sold two more and then announced that the raffle was closed.

I put all the entry forms in the box, stirred them up and asked a little girl who was standing there to select a name. She pulled out an entry form and handed it to me.

"The winner is Donald Lathrop," I announced.

"Mr. Lathrop," Norm exclaimed, "the industrial arts teacher at school."

I looked around and saw Mr. Lathrop coming forward.

"This is great, he said, "I have been wanting one of these for beginning wood working, but we never had the funds to buy it."

The crowd applauded as I handed Mr. Lathrop the saw and the packing box. I put the money in my pocket and then helped Norm pack up the toys he hadn't sold.

"That was a marvelous idea you had," I told Norm as we left.

When I got home, I counted the money. I had taken in twenty eight dollars which meant I had made a profit. But the best thing was that I won't have Mother bugging me to build more little shelves.

20 • Ring the Bell

WHY THERE WAS NO SUNDAY SERMON

People in Waupun still talk about the Sunday morning when traffic in the city was gridlocked. Members of Emanuel thought it was a minor inconvenience, but it ended up making most church goers in Waupun late for Sunday services.

I better explain what happened.

It all started one evening last winter. We had just finished saying our table prayer at supper, when Dad began.

"I sure got a surprise at the church council meeting last night," Dad reported.

"Did you get a raise?" Phil asked.

"No," Dad chuckled, "nothing that good."

"What was the surprise then?" Helene wanted to know. Helene liked surprises.

"Well," Dad began, "Matt Schielmann has an idea for the church picnic, which sounds like it could be a lot of fun."

Matt was a new member of Emanuel. He and his wife Rose had moved to the Village from Milwaukee when he retired from the Milwaukee Police Department.

"How come you decided to move to the Village?" Dad asked when they joined the congregation.

"Well, Rose's family originally settled here when they first came from Germany, and although she never lived here, she always thought of it as home," Matt answered.

"My grandparents are buried here, and we used to to visit their graves," Rose explained. "The Village always seemed nice and peaceful."

"And that is what appealed to me," Matt added. "After 30 years on the Milwaukee Police Force, I was really looking forward to peace and quiet."

"I just hope it isn't too quiet for you," Dad laughed, mentioning that he and the family had also moved to the Village from Milwaukee. "But you will find it peaceful."

Matt and Rose became active in the Village. Matt joined the volunteer fire department and the sheriff's auxiliary. Rose was soon active in the Thursday Women's Club and the Music Club.

At the annual meeting of the congregation, Matt was elected to the church council.

"That is something," Dad noted. "Usually it's the same group on the council."

Now about the church picnic. Next to the Christmas Eve program, the church picnic was the other event that kids in the congregation looked forward to with great expectation.

The picnic was held at the county park, located just outside of Waupun, about ten miles from the Village. Waupun was a city of some six thousand residents.

The church picnic took place at the conclusion of Vacation Bible School. Bible school was held the first three weeks after school let out. Each morning, the children of the congregation would gather in the church basement. They would memorize hymns and Bible verses and work on craft projects.

"Matt thinks it would be fun to have a parade of cars from the church to the picnic. He said they did that at his congregation in Milwaukee," Dad explained. "He said he thinks we could get a police escort since he's a volunteer with the sheriff's department."

"What did the council think of the idea?" Mother asked.

"They felt that if Matt was willing to do the work, and it wouldn't cost any money, it was OK with them," Dad answered.

At the next council meeting, Matt reported that he had talked with Leo Flannery, the sheriff's deputy who lived in the Village.

"Leo said he would be glad to do it," Dad later told us. "He said he could lead the procession and still get back to the Village for ten o'clock mass." Leo and his family were faithful members of the Village Catholic church.

A couple weeks later at supper, Dad brought us up to date on plans for the church picnic.

"I'll tell you Matt is getting everybody excited about the picnic. He met with the Sunday School teachers the other night, and they're going to go all out to be sure there are games for all the kids.

"He is really getting people enthusiastic about the picnic. Now he thinks we ought to have a band for the service. I told him I thought there were enough musicians in the congregation that we could have a good band. I know the church used to have a band. There's a whole bunch of band music in the storage closet. Would you be willing to play?" he asked Phil and me.

"Sure," we said, "it sounds like fun."

Soon about a dozen of us were practicing every week. Some of us were in the school band, but there were other members of the congregation who also played.

"I haven't played the clarinet since I graduated from high school," Herb Schmuhl told us, "so don't get upset if I come up with a few squeaks."

"And I haven't played my trumpet since high school either," said Fritz Freimark, "and I graduated a few years before you did."

"Don't worry," Dad said to them at the first practice. Dad was directing the band. "You'll do just fine."

Dad told us that we would play for the outdoor church service, accompanying the hymns and playing the prelude and postlude. "And let me dig through the music. Maybe we can find some old pieces to play in the afternoon."

The church picnic began with an outdoor service in the park band shell. This was followed by a potluck dinner and then an afternoon of games.

School ended, Bible School started. The three weeks flew by, and it was time for the church picnic.

The Sunday of the picnic came—a beautiful sunny day.

"You couldn't ask for better weather," said Mother at the breakfast table. She had gotten up early to be sure we were all ready for the picnic.

The congregation members had been instructed to come to the church for the parade to the park. There was a little grumbling from some of the members who lived east of the Village on the way to Waupun.

"Seems like a waste of time to come to the church and then drive back past our house," Fred Hammerschmidt complained.

"Oh, Fritz, it's no big deal," his wife chided him "Besides, the children want to be part of the parade."

Matt was out by the church before anyone else was there. Dad went to talk with him.

"Look what I have, Reverend," he said. There was a box of small American flags which could be attached to the car windows.

"I got a good deal on these at the Army surplus store in Fond du Lac," he told Dad. "This will be Rose's and my contribution to the picnic."

Matt explained the organization to Dad.

"Leo will lead the parade. You will follow Leo, then Charlie Rhindfresch, the congregation president, and then the rest of the congregation will follow. Why don't you get your car out and park it in front of the church? I'll place people as they come. Leo gave me a police light for my car, and I'll be at the end so anyone behind us will know there is a reason for the long procession."

Dad backed our Chevy out of the barn behind the parsonage and pulled in front of the church.

"Park right here, Reverend," he told Dad. "I'll start lining up the people when they come. Let's put a flag on your window."

Cars began pulling up to the church and Matt was busy lining them up.

"Here,"he told me, "why don't you give flags to everyone."

I began handing out the flags, showing people how to fasten them on their side windows.

The line of cars grew longer.

"Well, the Gruemanns just arrived," said Charlie. "If they're here, everyone is here."

The Gruemann family was notorious in the congregation for being late for everything.

"I don't know what it is with those people," Dad would fume. If you start something at 7 o'clock, they'll arrive at 7:15. f you move the time to 7:30, they'll come at 7:45."

"Relax, Henry," Mother would say, "it's their problem, not yours."

Matt had pulled his car in back of the Gruemann's and then walked to the front of the line.

"I wonder where Leo is. He should be here by now," he said to Dad,

"It's not like him to be late," Dad agreed.

Just then, Fred Conrad, our neighbor who lived across the street, came out of his house and walked up to Dad.

"Leo just called me," he told Dad. "He tried calling you, but figured you probably would be outside, so he called me and asked me to tell you that he's been called to an emergency over on the other side of Ripon. He radioed the sheriff's department and asked them to send a deputy over. He should be here shortly."

Most of the drivers were standing beside their cars. Dad went to Charlie, told him the news and asked him to relay the message to the drivers behind him.

Matt meanwhile was trying to be reassuring to Dad "He should be here any minute," Matt said. Matt didn't let on that he was worried. The procession had all been his idea, and now this had to happen.

In a few minutes, a sheriff's squad car pulled up and a uniformed deputy got out.

"Sorry to be late," he said to Dad and Matt. "I'm just not acquainted with the western end of the county. I usually patrol over on the east side. I'm Deputy O'Gara."

Dad and Matt introduced themselves.

"You're with the auxiliary, aren't you" he said to Matt. "You got a red light on your car?"

Matt nodded.

"OK," he said,"you pull up and park on the highway with the red light flashing and I'll lead the cars. We're heading for the Waupun park, right?"

Dad said yes as he got in the car.

Phil was driving and Dad sat in the passenger side. Mother, Helene and I were in the back seat.

"All right, let's go," called the deputy.

"Now, Phil, you be careful and don't run into the police car," Mother called from the back. I could see Phil scowl as he replied "Yes, Mother. I'll be careful."

Why There Was No Sunday Sermon • 25

The cars turned right onto the state highway following the squad car.

"Do you suppose he'll blow his siren?" Helene asked.

"I doubt it," Dad answered. "There's no need for that. Look back and see the big line of cars."

We looked back and saw a long line of cars, American flags flying briskly.

"I can't even see Mr. Schielmann's car," I said.

"He must be there," Phil said.

We were soon nearing the entrance to the county park.

"He's not turning into the park," Phil exclaimed as the squad car kept going straight past the entrance pillars on the road to the park.

"Just keep going. He may be going to use the back entrance to the park," Dad said.

Dad looked back. All the cars were following; none had turned into the park. Good Germans, Dad thought—they just follow the leader.

When the back entrance to the park came up, Phil slowed down, expecting the deputy to turn. But he just kept going straight.

"Blow the horn at him, Phil," Dad said, "let's get his attention, so we can get turned around."

Phil began beeping the horn just as the cars entered the city of Waupun. Charlie in the car behind ours couldn't figure out why we hadn't turned into the park or why the pastor's car was beeping its horn.

"Maybe we're supposed to have a little parade or something," said Charlie to his wife "Well, I suppose I may as well beep my horn too."

The driver behind him heard Charlie and the pastor sounding their horns, so he began beeping as well. The rest of the drivers joined in. As the long column of cars drove down Waupun's Main Street, all the cars were beeping their horns.

There weren't a lot of people on Waupun's Main Street at that hour of Sunday morning. But those who were there, stopped and stared as they saw the the parade of beeping cars, American flags flying and red lights flashing on the deputy's squad car.

"What in the world is going on?" Dad wondered. "Phil, stop at the stop light and let me out I'll run up and talk with Deputy O'Gara."

At the stoplight, Dad got out and ran to the deputy's car.

"Where are you taking us?" he asked.

"You're going to the Waupun City Park, aren't you?" Deputy O'Gara replied

"No, we're going to the county park," Dad told him.

"Oh," he answered, "we went by that didn't we?"

Dad nodded.

"OK, no problem. We'll just take a left at the next light, go around the block and head back to the entrance."

Dad walked back to the car. The horns had stopped by this time and members were sitting in their cars, wondering what was happening.

Dad motioned for the cars to follow him and the squad car. That should have been the end of things except...well, except that the next light was the north-south state highway and there, stopping traffic was a National Guard military police jeep.

"Now what?" asked Mother.

"I read in the paper that the Wisconsin National Guard is traveling to Camp McCoy today for its annual training," Phil said. "We must have hit one of the convoys."

"Guess all we can do is wait," Dad said. "I'll skip the sermon today, and we'll just have the children's portion of the service."

We sat and waited. What we didn't know was that behind us, the early service at Immanuel Lutheran Church had just gotten out, and people were trying to turn on to Main Street from the church parking lot. However, they couldn't turn because our members' cars were blocking the street.

Meanwhile, the early mass at St. Joseph's had let out. Half their members were trying to turn on to the north south state highway, but couldn't because it was blocked with the National Guard convoy. The other half were trying to get on the east-west highway, but couldn't because it was filled with the cars from our church, and cars heading for the nine-thirty service at the First Reformed Church....plus the normal traffic on the state highway. Then cars began arriving trying to get to the Methodist church for their service. Every driver seemed to want to go a different direction, but not one could move. Total gridlock ensued.

Finally the slow moving guard convoy cleared the intersection, the MP's moved on, and Deputy O'Gara motioned for us to follow the squad car. Everyone tried to moving at the same time. A Waupun City policeman came up to Deputy O'Gara's squad car and asked what was going on. Deputy O'Gara explained, and the city policeman worked to get our procession turned around

It was slow getting everyone through the intersection since traffic had been backed up both ways plus all the church members were trying to get in and out of the church parking lots.

Finally after a good twenty minutes, all the Emanuel members got turned around and headed to the park. As I looked back, I could see cars still stopped in all directions.

"I sure apologize for this," the deputy told Dad and Matt at the park. "I just don't know this end of the county. I thought sure you were going to the Waupun City Park. I"ve got to go back now and help the Waupun police straighten out the traffic jam there."

The church service went well. The congregation sang lustily with the band accompaniment. The Bible School children recited their Bible verses and sang the hymns they had memorized. No one seemed disappointed when Dad announced that because of the delay, he was omitting the sermon. (Later at home, Mother said, "At least they didn't applaud.")

Then it was time for dinner. There may be better meals than the church picnic potluck dinner, but I can't remember many.

What an array of food! There was fried chicken, home-smoked ham, pork chops, sauerbraten and a dozen different kinds of hot dishes. There was an endless array of salads: two-bean salad, three-bean salad, four-bean salad, cole slaw, lettuce and more. And Jell-O of every color plus my favorite—whipped Jell-O. Then there were the desserts: all kinds of pies including strawberry, rhubarb, lemon meringue, coconut cream, and more. And cakes, cookies and tortes. No one made better tortes than German women, Dad often commented.

One advantage of being the preacher's son was that our family always got to go first at events like this. But before we could eat, we had the table prayer.

Dad stood on the table and in his loudest voice said "We'll sing the table prayer. I think you all know it."

Years later I learned that the prayer we sang had been written by Methodist Charles Wesley and set to music by a German Reformed composer, but we Lutherans had adopted it as our own and we forcefully sang

"Be present at our table, Lord.

"Be here and everywhere adored.

"These mercies bless and grant that we

"May feast in paradise with thee. Amen."

Hardly had the "Amen" died out when the two lines started moving down the picnic tables where the food was laid out. Members of the Ladies Aid hovered nearby removing empty dishes and replacing them with full ones.

The last of the diners filed through as the first ones through the line started coming back for seconds and desserts.

"You know, Alfred, I think church picnics are better than most threshing meals," I heard Hans Buettemann say to his friend Al Schoenweiss.

The grown-ups were having their second cups of coffee, and the kids were starting to fidget when Willard Monk, the Sunday School superintendent, climbed on a picnic table to announce the afternoon events.

"OK, everyone, let me have your attention" he called in his loudest voice. People quieted down. "First, I want to thank Matt Schielman for organizing the procession today. We had a little more excitement than we had planned on, but we all got here safely and soundly. Let's have a big hand for Matt."

Loud applause filled the air. (I could see Dad leaning over and saying something to Mother. Later Dad told us he was sure relieved that people liked it because Matt had worked so hard.)

"And Matt asked that you all turn in your flags so we can use them again next year," Willard continued after the applause died down.

"Every student gets two tickets. You can redeem them for pop, ice cream or candy bars at the stand which the church council is running. Grown ups can buy treats if they have any room after that great dinner.

"The Sunday School teachers are setting up the games now. We'll start with the preschoolers, then the primary and then the older grades. There will be games for every age and prizes for all. And at two o'clock, we have something new. It's a ball game between the high schoolers and the adults."

The games began. Mollie Monk who taught the pre schoolers asked all of her students to gather around.

"Our first game is the penny hunt," she told them. She pointed to a large a canvas tarpaulin with a mound of saw dust and wood shavings in the middle. "There are a bunch of pennies hidden here. There is also one quarter. When I say 'Go' you can start hunting for the pennies and the quarter. You get to keep all the coins you find."

Several mothers quickly looked at their children's Sunday clothes and wished they had remembered to bring everyday clothes.

"Too late now," I heard one say.

The children gathered at the edge of the tarpaulin, waiting for the command to start.

"OK, you have ten minutes. Ready, set, go." Hardly had the words gotten out of her mouth when the horde of little ones dove into the pile.

"I found one," said Jimmy Kohlbar, holding up a shiny penny for his mother to see.

"Good," his mother replied, "keep looking."

More pennies were found as sawdust flew through the air like a desert sand storm. Suddenly a loud scream came from the busy diggers. Everyone stopped.

"I found it, I found it," screeched Joannie Hessler, holding up a shiny 25 cent piece. "I found the quarter!"

She quickly ran to her mother, gave her the quarter and said "Hold this for me, please. And don't lose it."

"I won't," her smiling mother assured her.

Mollie clapped her hands and said, "OK, children, one minute more and then it's time for the fish pond."

There was a frantic pawing through the sawdust in a search for any remaining coins.

"That's it," Mollie called. "Everyone out. Dust yourself off and then line up for the fish pond."

The fish pond had neither fish nor water. Rather, the children were handed a stick with a piece of string attached to it. There was a blanket hung between two trees . The child threw the line over the blanket and a Sunday School teacher attached a small gift, gave the string a tug and the child lifted up the stick to receive the gift.

Squeals came forth as each child caught a "fish" and proudly ran to a parent to show the gift.

The games continued as the time came for the older children to participate. There were all sorts of contests. There was the three-legged race where teams of two would tie their middle legs together and at the word "Go" would awkwardly race toward the finish line. The winners were usually the pair who avoided falling; although this rarely happened.

Then there was the bag race. Contestants were handed burlap feed bags. They would put their feet in the bag, pull the bags up to their waists and would attempt to hop to the finish line. This was followed by the wheelbarrow race. One contestant would stand on his hands while his partner picked up the other person's feet and attempted to drive the person like a wheelbarrow.

Hardly had this race ended, when it was time for the cracker eating contest. Participants were given six soda crackers. The object was to eat them as quickly as possible and the first contestant who could whistle was the winner. Whistling, it turned out, was no small feat after a mouthful of dry soda crackers.

On the ball diamond, the game between the high schoolers and the adults was in full swing. The adults were no match for the young people who had a number of high school players on the team.

As the games went on, there was a steady parade of boys and girls to the stand where they were exchanging their tickets for treats.

Soon it was nearing four o'clock, the ending time for the picnic. Since most of the members were dairy farmers, they had to get back home, change clothes and milk the cows.

Dads began calling to their children while their wives were gathering up their pans from the potluck dinner.

As people began to leave, Mrs. Stroessenreuter began asking "Has anyone seen LeRoy?"

We also started asking around. Where had he gone? Who saw him last?

LeRoy was a fifth grader and was always going off by himself.

"I think I saw him over by the swimming pool a while back," someone called.

"He didn't have his swimming suit, so I'm sure he's not in the pool," his mother said. "I just hope he didn't wander off in the woods."

The park had forty acres of woodland with trails and camping sites. Several boys volunteered to see if he had gone there.

"What about the river?" someone asked.

"No need to worry about that," one of the men assured the questioner. "The Rock River is only a foot deep over by the golf course."

"I remember seeing him walking over toward the golf course," one of the girls said. "I told him to look out that he didn't get hit on the head with a golf ball."

As people were standing around talking and wondering what to do next, LerRoy suddenly appeared.

"Where in the world have you been?" his mother wanted to know. "I was worried silly."

"Over there," he gestured, pointing toward the country club. "I was just walking around. Look what I found."

He reached into his pocked and pulled out three golf balls.

"Where did you find them?" one of the boys want to know.

"They were just laying there on the lawn, "LeRoy answered, "right by a little flag."

DAD AND THE SINGING HOLLANDERS

The phone rang just as we were finishing supper.

"Now who could that be?" Mother wondered.

Mother had this thing about the phone. If she wasn't expecting a call, she would look at the phone, wondering who might be calling. Sometimes the phone would ring five or six times while she stood there, listing who it might be.

"I hope it isn't bad news. What if someone died?" she might say. Or "I hope it isn't Mrs. Gehrke. She always talks for an hour."

We kids would usually say something to the effect of "For heavens sake, pick up the phone and find out."

She was the same about the mail. If a letter came from someone she wasn't expecting to hear from, she would hold the letter in hand, staring at it. If it were from her sister, and it wasn't her turn to write, Mother would get anxious.

"Oh, dear, I hope no one is sick."

Or if it came from one of her brothers, she might say something like "Why Alfred never writes. This must really be serious."

As Mother was pondering who might be calling, Dad got up, went into the dining room to the phone and answered it.

We could hear him from the kitchen.

"Yes. This is he. No, this is fine."

A silence followed.

"Just a moment. Let me get my calendar."

Dad put the phone down, went into his study and came back with his pocket calendar where he kept all his appointments.

"Tomorrow evening looks fine. How about seven o'clock? Use the door to my study. That would be the door on the right as you face the house. Fine, I'll see you tomorrow evening."

Dad talked a little longer, hung up the phone and came back to the table. We waited expectantly to see who would be coming to see him. Usually calls like this would be from a member who was planning to get married, and she and her fiancé would come to make arrangements. Or it might be a member wanting to talk with Dad about a private matter. But judging from the tone in Dad's voice, it didn't sound like he had been talking with a member of the church.

"Well," he said, sitting down before we had our evening devotions, "that was interesting ."

"Who was it?" Mother wanted to know.

"It was Herman Rietsma," Dad answered.

Herman Riestma, I thought. He ran the hardware store in the Village and was a member of the Reformed Church. Why would he want to see Dad?

"What in the world did he want?" Mother asked.

"Herman and a couple of members of the Alto Christian Reformed Church are coming to see me tomorrow evening. They want to know if I would be interested in directing the church's male chorus," Dad answered.

"Why you can't do that. You're busy on Sundays," Mother told him (as though Dad might need to be reminded).

"No, it's not a church choir. They don't sing at services. They're a group of men from the church who like to sing. I think most of the Dutch churches have men's choruses," Dad told her.

I probably should explain about the Dutch Reformed churches in the area. Next to the Germans, the Dutch—generally called Hollanders—were the largest ethnic group in the Village and surrounding area. Most of them were members of the Reformed Church, a Calvinistic Protestant denomination. Like the Lutherans, there were several varieties of the Reformed Church. The Village had a congregation of the Reformed Church in America. East of the Village was the small community of Alto which had two Reformed churches: the Reformed Church in America and the Christian Reformed Church. Both branches were rather strict. There was no unnecessary work on the Sabbath. Services were held twice on Sunday, morning and evening. Drinking was frowned on; although in communities which had a sizable Dutch population, many of the taverns had doors at the back, so patrons could enter without being seen. These were often referred to as "Dutch Doors." Most businesses in the Village were closed on Sunday; although Miller's Drug was open in the morning so people could buy their Sunday papers and get ice cream for Sunday dinners.

Anyway, Dad got along real well with the Reformed members. He was friends with the Reformed pastor in the Village. The call from Mr. Rietsma was a little surprising, but we didn't see anything out of the ordinary about it. After all, Dad had a reputation as a good musician. He directed the choirs at church, he was a skilled organist and he periodically was a vocal soloist at civic events.

The next evening after supper, Dad brought a couple of extra chairs to his study, closed the door, turned on the outside light and waited for the group to arrive. The rest of the family sat in the living room. The Venetian blinds were open just a crack so we could see out.

At two minutes before seven, Mr. Rietsma's black Chevrolet pulled up in front of the parsonage. Four men got out.

"Good grief, it looks like they're all going to a funeral," said Phil as he watched them come to the study door. They were all dressed in black suits, with white shirts and dark ties.

"Why don't you kids go to your rooms," Mother suggested as she heard a knock on the door to the study.

We complied, figuring we would learn what had happened.

It wasn't too long before Helene came to my room and said, "I think we can go downstairs now. I just saw them drive away."

Helene's bedroom faced the front of the house, and she had been keeping an eye on the car.

"They left," she reported.

We trooped downstairs to the living room and waited for Dad to come out of the study.

"Well," said Mother when he came out.

"That should work out just fine," Dad answered. He proceeded to tell us that the chorus met on Thursday evenings from September through May. Rehearsals ran about an hour and a half.

"Actually, the rehearsals run about an hour, but they stop for coffee about halfway through," he said.

The Hollanders were big coffee drinkers and took coffee breaks in the morning and afternoon, long before it became normal for most people.

"The men from the Village will give me a ride to rehearsals. They have an annual concert at their church plus a joint concert with the other men's choruses from the area. Oh, yes, they sing in church one Sunday a year, but I don't have to be there. And, they pay ten dollars for each rehearsal and concert."

Mother brightened up immediately.

"That's pretty generous," she exclaimed.

"They seem to have plenty of money. Every member pays weekly dues to belong."

"Oh," Dad remembered, "they agreed that I would select the music. I'm not interested in just conducting Gospel tunes."

"Don't forget, you have all that music from the men's chorus in Milwaukee," Mother reminded him.

I remember Dad telling us when we lived in Milwaukee that Uncle Carl and he sang in a men's chorus. It was conducted by a well-known choral director who came to Milwaukee every week from Chicago to direct the group. Dad and Uncle Carl often talked about how much they enjoyed this.

"Yes, I thought of that," Dad answered. "I'll have to dig out that music and see if they're able to handle it."

So began Dad's directing.

From time to time Dad would report on how things were going.

"There are a lot of good singers there. Most haven't had any musical training, but they seem willing to learn," he mentioned. "I've started with some easy pieces, and I'll gradually add more difficult numbers."

One day Dad was especially excited after rehearsal.

"Last night I got them to try Bach's 'Jesu, Priceless Treasure,'" he said. "They seemed to like it."

Rehearsals continued. It was nearing the time for the joint concert. Choruses from both the Reformed Churches in America and the Christian Reformed congregations participated.

"The two church groups have a number of differences, but they seem to be able to get along when it comes to singing," Dad told us one night at supper. "They're better than the Lutherans that way."

The joint concert would be held in the Waupun Auditorium. Eight choruses would sing. Each one would perform three numbers and then all the groups would join for a closing number.

Dad had selected three numbers: the old Gospel hymn "Let Us Gather at the River," Noble Cain's arrangement of "Rise Up, Oh Men of God" and finally Bach's "Jesu, Priceless Treasure."

Dad reported that he thought the concert went well. "Our group sounded the best I've ever heard them."

The following week after rehearsal, Dad had gave us this report at supper.

"Well, I don't know if I'll have a job with the chorus next year," he remarked.

"Why do you say that?" Mother asked.

"It seems that some of the men from the other choruses started needling our chorus members. They were calling them the 'High Brow Hollanders.'"

We all laughed. We thought that was funny.

"Why would they say that?" Mother wanted to know.

"I guess maybe the Bach number was a little too much for some of the other choruses. Our men seemed to like it OK. But you know how sensitive people can be on things like that." Dad responded.

The following week after rehearsal, Dad was all smiles.

"The men told me they had a special meeting of the chorus after church on Sunday morning. They decided that being called the 'High Brow Hollanders' was actually a compliment. One of the men said that back in Reformation times, the Reformed were called Protestants as an insulting term, but they adopted it as a name of honor. The chorus unanimously voted to keep me as director," Dad reported.

Rehearsals continued. Dad introduced other numbers including including a selection from Handel's *Messiah*.

The annual concert had a big audience at the church. Our family had received a special invitation, and we were shown to seats of honor in the front.

During intermission, Mr. Rietsma went to the lectern.

"Last summer the chorus decided to ask Reverend Kurtz if he would direct our group. I think I speak for all the members when I say that we have not only enjoyed singing for him, but we have learned a lot about music. We took up a collection and would like to present Reverend Kurtz with this gift certificate as a token of appreciation."

He motioned for Dad to come up and then ended him an envelope.

Dad shook hands with him, thanked him and the chorus and told the audience how much he enjoyed directing the chorus and what a great bunch of singers they were. There was loud applause.

The next fall, Dad again directed the chorus, introducing some additional numbers. For the joint concert, he decided they would do "For Unto Us a Child is Born" from *Messiah*, the concluding chorus from Bach's "Nun Dunket Alle Gott" and an arrangement of the old Dutch hymn "We Gather Together."

Dad suggested that we might like to attend the concert.

"You'll probably be the only Lutherans in the audience, but I think you will enjoy it," he told us.

We rode with Dad to Waupun, some ten miles from the Village. Phil had to work that evening, so Mother, Helene and I went with Dad.

We found seats toward the back of the auditorium.

"No reserved seats for us this time," I said to Mother.

"Shh," Mother said. "We don't want to be conspicuous."

"What does 'conspicuous' mean?" Helene wanted to know.

Mother again said "Shh," and added, "I'll tell you later."

The concert seemed to go on and on. Except for Dad's chorus, most of the music sounded pretty much the same.

After the concert was over, we waited around for Dad. I noticed he was talking to a man.

"I wonder who that is," I said to Mother. "He isn't a chorus member, and he doesn't look like one of the Reformed preachers."

In a few minutes Dad joined us, and we went out to the car When we got in, before I could ask about the man, Helene demanded "OK, now what does conspicuous mean and why shouldn't we be that, whatever it is?"

We all laughed and Helene got indignant.

"What's so funny, just because I don't know what a word means?"

Mother explained that since our family were the only Lutherans in the audience, she didn't want to draw attention to us by parading up in front.

This satisfied Helene, and I changed the subject by asking who Dad had been talking to at the end of the concert.

"That was very interesting," Dad answered. "He's what they call a field man for Calvin College."

"The college has a farmer?" Helene asked.

Again we laughed, and again Helene was indignant.

"Farmers work in fields," she pointed out.

"Well," Dad said, "this is a different kind of field. It means he goes out and talks with people and congregations who might be interested in Calvin College."

Dad explained that Calvin College was located in Grand Rapids, Michigan, and was supported by the Christian Reformed Church.

"The choir I direct is a part of the Christian Reformed Church," Dad explained. "Anyway, he told me he was quite impressed with the singing of our our chorus. He told me that at Christmas time, Calvin College presents Handel's *Messiah*, and the college invites various church choirs to be in the chorus. He asked if our chorus would be interested in singing there."

"What did you tell him?" Mother asked.

"I told him that this sounded great, but I couldn't answer for the chorus, especially since I was a Lutheran pastor."

"Did you feel conspicuous?" Helene wanted to know.

"No, but I told him to send a letter to Mr. Rietsma, and it would be up to the chorus to decide."

There was no chorus rehearsal the next week. Members took the week off after their big concert. A week later after the next rehearsal that Dad reported on the invitation the chorus had received.

"The men were really excited about the invitation. It was the first time any chorus in this area had ever been invited to sing. I gather that in this is quite an honor," Dad told us.

"Are they going? Will you go too?" Mother asked.

"No, I won't be going. The men are trying to figure out if they can make the trip. Most of them are dairy farmers, and it is difficult for them to get away. The way they were talking it sounds as though some of the men will stay home and take care of the milking so others can go. My guess is that more than half of them will be able to make the trip."

Dad added that since the *Messiah* presentation was in December, they had about six months to make arrangements.

"But there's no doubt that they will go. It means that we'll have to do a lot of rehearsing which means I'll really have to prepare as well. Aside from 'For Unto Us a Child is Born,' I've never directed anything from *Messiah*."

A week later at the supper table, Dad gave a report.

"It looks as though about fifteen of the chorus members will be able to go. The farmers have made arrangements either to have chorus members do their milking or have family members take care of things. We decided that the whole chorus will practice selections from" *Messiah* and do a special Christmas concert at the church."

Never had a group practiced harder. Rather than take the summer off, the chorus continued practicing throughout June, July and August...except when our family went on vacation.

"The extra income will come in handy," Mother remarked.

Summer turned into autumn. Dad would walk around the house, humming selections from Handel.

"Well, the men have things figured out. They decided they will go in three cars. Some of them have relatives down in South Holland near Chicago, so they will drive there the first night stay overnight and then head to Grand Rapids. There are a couple of rehearsals and then three concerts on Thursday, Friday and Saturday nights. On Monday, they'll drive straight home," Dad said.

"Why don't they leave on Sunday and get home sooner?"Mother asked.

"Oh, no," Dad explained, "with the Christian Reformed, there's no traveling on Sunday. They'll stay and go to church and then leave bright and early on Monday."

Everything went according to schedule. At the next chorus rehearsal, Dad got a full report.

"This was one of the biggest adventures most of these men had. Some of them had never been out of Wisconsin before. Things went great. They had a wonderful time and. . ."

Dad got up, went to his study and came back with the program.

"Look at this. Here's how the chorus asked to be listed on the program.

We all looked at the program. There it was

"The High Brow Hollanders, Alto, Wisconsin."

THE MYSTERY AT THE GAS STATION

Crime was not a major problem in the Village. Old timers would talk about when people "thought" that Jesse James and his gang had ridden through the Village, but since they hadn't tried to rob the bank, no one was certain if indeed the notorious band of criminals had been there.

Then there was the time back in the 1930's when the John Dillinger gang had stopped at the Texaco station. At least, that's what people thought. The way they told it was that one afternoon this big car with Illinois license plates pulled into the station. They parked the car at the side of the driveway, and a woman got out to use the restroom. They didn't buy any gas, but the people in the station noticed there were three or four men in the car.

"Looked to me like it could have been the Dillinger gang heading up to northern Wisconsin," said one of the guys who was at the station. Of course, no one knew for sure.

"I sure wasn't going to go out and ask them," he said later.

But criminal activity was virtually unknown. The Village had no police force. Wes Carley was the Village constable, but this was only a part-time duty for him since his main job was being the Village maintenance man. He plowed the streets in winter, mowed the park lawn in summer, collected trash year around and maintained the Village hall.

The only reported criminal event in recent memory really wasn't a crime at all, but resulted in a degree of hilarity for residents of the Village. It involved the disappearance of Willard Monk's '39 Ford.

Willard was the Sunday School superintendent at Emanuel. He and his wife Mollie lived in a small house just west of the

Village business section. Willard worked at Herb Schmuhl's grocery and dry goods store, and Mollie was a clerk in the post office. Both jobs were located a few hundred feet from their home, so they always walked to work. Their car would sit in the garage, often going unused for weeks at a time.

One Thursday evening they had been invited to have supper with Mollie's cousin and his wife who lived out in the country. Willard went to the garage to get the car. To his amazement it was gone.

He ran into the house, excitedly calling to Mollie, "Our car has been stolen! I've got to call Wes."

Wes had just gotten home from his Village duties when he got Willard's excited call. Willard quickly explained the situation and asked Wes, "Should I call Leo Flannery?" Leo was the county deputy who lived in the Village and was called upon if there appeared to be real criminal activity.

"Relax, Willard," Wes said. "Your car hasn't been stolen. It's sitting in the Lutheran church parking lot, right where you left it on Sunday."

Then he remembered. Willard was the Sunday School superintendent at Emanuel, and he liked to get to church early to make sure everything was set for the session. It had been raining when he left in the morning, so he drove to the church and parked his car in the lot. By the time Sunday School and morning services were over, the rain had stopped and the sun was shining, so Willard and Mollie walked home, oblivious to the fact that their car was standing in the church lot.

Now that's the kind of criminal activity which the Village would typically face. What took place one Saturday night was really out of the ordinary. Let me tell you what happened.

It was after nine o'clock on Saturday night when Phil came home from his job at the filling station. On alternate Saturday nights, he worked alone and was responsible for closing the station.

When Phil got home on Saturday nights, he would be tired from a full day's work. He would have a snack and go to bed. I was in the kitchen when he came in. Mother was upstairs, getting Helene ready for bed. Dad was in his study with the door closed. Sometimes he would be working on his sermon. Other times he would be reading. On occasion, I knew that he might be sneaking in a game of solitaire. Mother didn't know about that, and Dad had warned me not to say anything about it to her. Mother thought there was something sinful about playing cards, especially on a Saturday night when he should be working on his sermon.

"You look worried," I said to Phil as he pulled up a chair at the kitchen table and sat down.

"I had kind of a strange experience tonight," he told me. "As I was getting ready to close, a couple of guys came in. I didn't know them. They bought a dollar's worth of gas and hung around for a while, like they were looking the place over."

"Then what happened?" I asked.

"Well, nothing. One guy bought two Mars bars and watched carefully when I took out the key to open the candy cupboard."

"Mars bars? They're expensive. And two of them!" I said. All other candy bars were a nickel. However, Mars bars were a dime, and rarely did many people buy one and never two.

Before I tell you more, I should explain about the station. The filling station or service station was located directly back of the church. It was owned by Augie Kohls. Augie and his wife had no children, but over the years the young men Augie had hired to work at the station became almost an extended family for them.

Augie was very particular about who worked there. The high school student he hired had to have excellent grades, be well respected by the faculty and plan to attend college. As a result, former employees tended to be a successful group.

During vacations, they would return to visit. If things got busy, they would help out. In the summer, Augie would hire one of the former workers to run the station while he and his wife went on vacation. It was not unusual to have a Ph.D. washing a customer's windshield.

The alumni, as they were frequently called, went on to college and successful careers. A couple of them became school superintendents, others were teachers; a couple were business people; and one became a minister. The only exception was the son of the former pastor at Emanuel. He so thoroughly enjoyed his work at the station that he become an auto mechanic, . . . much to his father's consternation because he had hoped his son would follow in his footsteps and become a pastor.

The station had been built in the late 1920's when Spanish architecture was popular. The two buildings had a stucco finish and a faux tile roof. One building was where oil changes and minor repairs were done. The other building had the office, storage areas, a large waiting room with chairs and a pop machine. One distinctive feature was the women's restroom. Augie used to say that it was the most attractive public restroom in Wisconsin. In addition to the toilet facilities, it had a waiting area with wicker furniture. During the summer, Augie always put fresh flowers there.

The Village was on a main highway to several resort lakes. It was about one tank of gas from Chicago to the station, and the women's restroom was a major draw for business on Friday nights during the summer.

The station was a favorite gathering place for kids and neighbors. It was especially interesting to be there when the alumni were home during vacations. One could learn all sorts of things about college life, jobs and what was happening in the Village.

But getting back to Phil's concern.

"So what happened?" I asked.

"Nothing. They stood around for a while. The one guy ate both his candy bars. They saw me look at the clock a couple of times and finally one said, 'I suppose you're getting ready to close.' I told him that yes, I was, so they left and drove off," Phil said.

"So, then what?" I asked.

"Nothing. I put the money in the downstairs safe, turned off the lights, locked up and came home," Phil answered.

"So why are you worried?"

"There was just something about these guys which didn't seem right. Why would two strangers hang around the station late on a Saturday night? I hope nothing happens. Well, I guess I'll have something to eat and go bed. I'm tired."

A little bit later I went to my room and got ready for bed. My room was at the back of the house, and the window over the head of my bed looked out over our back yard. I had a good view of the station from there.

I left my shade up that night. Usually I pulled it down since the sun would shine directly on my face in the morning. I thought if anything happens at the station, I might be able to see things from there.

I woke up a couple of times during the night. Each time, I would look intently at the station. Each time I failed to see anything but the dark buildings, faintly outlined by the street light.

After church on Sunday, Phil told me he was going to stop at the station and tell Augie about Saturday night and see if everything was OK. He came back in a few minutes and said Augie appreciated that he had told him about the two guys, and he would keep his eyes open for them.

I continued to keep my shade up for the next few nights, but there was nothing to be seen. I did get awakened early with the sun coming through the window, so I again pulled the shade down at night and forgot about keeping watch over the station.

I'm not certain what caused me to wake up one Saturday night. Maybe I had heard something. I raised the shade and looked out at the station. Things appeared normal, but then I thought I saw a glint of light through the station window.

I watched for a few minutes and didn't see the light again, but I thought I saw a car parked in the shadows near the entrance to the station driveway.

I decided to tell Phil and see what he thought. I quietly opened the door of my bedroom and tiptoed across the hall to Phil's bedroom. I didn't want to wake Mother who was a light sleeper and would immediately forbid us to leave the house.

I let myself into Phil's room and gently shook him awake. I told him what I thought I had seen.

"Let's check it out," he said. "Get dressed and we'll sneak over there. And be quiet so we don't wake Mother."

I ducked back to my room, quickly dressed and met Phil in the hall. We tiptoed down the steps, into the kitchen and let ourselves out the side door. Just before we went out the door, I saw the ice pick sitting on the ledge where we had used it a few days earlier when we made ice cream. I grabbed it and whispered to Phil,

"Just in case."

We silently moved through the shadows toward the station. We knew every inch of our back yard, and we kept close to the bushes on the side of the yard. When we got within sight of the big side window of the station, we stopped and watched.

"I saw a light. There's someone in there," Phil whispered.

"And there's a car over there," I whispered back.

"Let's go call the sheriff's department, " Phil said.

"Just a minute," I told him.

I crawled over to the car, ice pick in hand. I quickly punched each of the back tires, noted the license plate number and came back to where Phil was waiting.

"Let's go. Be real careful."

We hurriedly sneaked back into the house. Phil went to the telephone. He jiggled the hand set to get the operator's attention. The night operator would often doze off since few people made calls late at night.

In a minute, I heard a faint voice saying, "Number, please."

"This is Philip Kurtz. Can you call the sheriff's department right away? There are people in Augie Kohls' station."

This time the voice was louder.

"I'll call right away, and I'll also call Leo. And you stay away from the station until the police get there."

"I will," Phil promised.

Phil and I went out in the back yard just in time to see a car with its headlights off pull away from the station and head down the state highway.

A few minutes later Leo's squad car pulled up, and we ran over to it.

We quickly explained what had happened.

"Which way did they go?" Leo asked.

I pointed to the east.

"It's a dark-colored Plymouth, either a '41 or a '45. The license number is 563-335. I don't think they'll get too far," and I told Leo what I had done.

"That was a little bit dangerous, but smart" he told me. "I'll send out a radio alert."

He went into his car, and while he was talking, another squad car pulled up.

The deputy got out of his car, looked us over (apparently deciding we weren't the criminals) and walked over to Leo's car.

Leo got off the radio and told the deputy what had happened.

The Mystery at the Gas Station • 47

"I'll go down the highway, and if they are stopped with flat tires, I'll radio for backup, " the deputy said. "Check the station and see what you can find out."

The squad car took off.

"We should probably call Augie to let him know," Leo said.

"I'll go back to the house and call him," Phil said.

"Let's take a look at things," Leo said "but first I'll pull the squad car over to the door so I can hear the radio."

"Stay behind me and don't touch anything. I doubt if anyone is in there, but we need to be careful."

Leo picked up his flashlight, drew his revolver, and we walked to the front door. Leo reached in his pocket and pulled out a pair of gloves which he put on.

"There might be finger prints here," he said.

The front door was open, and there was broken glass in the door from the smashed door window.

"That's how they got in," Leo pointed out. "They reached in and undid the lock."

Leo looked around.

"No one here. Where are the light switches?" he asked.

I pointed to the switches over the pop cooler.

Leo switched them on, and we looked around the office. Just then Phil came in.

"Augie's on his way over," he told Leo.

The cash register had been pried open.

"That was a waste of time," Phil noted. "We never keep any money in there at night."

"What do you do with the money?" Leo asked.

"We put it downstairs in the safe," Phil said.

"We'll check that when Augie gets here," Leo said, continuing his search of the office area.

"Look, they broke into the candy case," I said. The glass on the case was shattered. I looked inside.

"It looks like the only thing they took were the Mars bars," I said.

"I bet it was the same guys," Phil responded.

"What guys were those?" Leo wanted to know.

Phil recounted what had happened earlier, including how one had bought two Mars bars.

"Can you describe them?" Leo wanted to know.

Just then a car pulled up in front. Augie got out and came into the station.

Leo explained what had happened.

"I don't think they're going to get too far," Leo said, "thanks to his quick thinking" pointing to me.

Augie smiled. "Good job, both of you."

"Why don't you check downstairs and see if they got into your safe," Leo told Augie.

Augie went down the stairs in the back store room. He reappeared shortly.

"Nope, they didn't get into the safe. I doubt if they found it."

Just then a voice came over the radio.

"Leo, I got them. I just called for backup to transport them to the county jail."

"Do you need me?" Leo asked.

"No," came the response. "When the other squad gets here, Ill come back and fill you in. I've got both guys handcuffed in the back seat. Here comes the other squad now. Ten four."

"Ten four," Leo replied.

"I'll get my camera and take pictures of the break-in," Leo said, "and I'll dust for fingerprints."

Leo went to his squad car and returned with a camera and a small black bag.

I watched carefully. I had read about evidence gathering, but had never seen it firsthand. Leo took pictures of the front door, the broken candy case and the cash register.

He took out a container of white powder from the bag and, with a small brush, dusted the door knobs, the cash register and the candy case.

"There are a lot of prints here. I'll need to get your prints so I can tell whose might be the intruders," he told Augie and Phil.

The Mystery at the Gas Station • 49

Phil was going to be fingerprinted. Wow, I thought, this is better than a detective story.

"Anything else look as though it has been disturbed or broken into?" Leo asked Augie.

Augie had been checking things out.

"Doesn't appear to be anything," he replied.

Just then the other squad car pulled up. The deputy got out and came into the station.

"Got everything, Leo?" he asked.

"I think so. The only thing we found missing was a box of Mars bars," Leo told him.

"And that was in the back seat of the car," the deputy answered.

"You can clean up the glass and board up the door," Leo told Augie. "I'll stop over tomorrow and finish the report. I'll have to get a statement from you too," he told us.

Phil and I walked back to the house.

"Should we wake Mother and Dad to tell them what happened?" I asked Phil.

"Let's wait until morning," he answered.

The next morning I heard Dad get up. I got up too and so did Phil.

We went downstairs and told Dad what had happened.

Mother heard our voices and came down, wondering why we had gotten up so early.

"You two could have been killed," Mother exclaimed after we told her the story.

"What do you mean, killed?" came a sleepy voice. Helene had come down the stairs just in time to hear Mother's comment.

We repeated the story.

"Wow," Helene said, "that was exciting. Next time will you wake me up, so I can come too?"

We smiled.

"I hope there will never be a next time," Phil answered.

"Shoot," answered Helene, "I miss out on everything."

On Monday afternoon, Leo stopped at the house and took a statement from us including Phil's description of the two guys who had been at the station earlier.

"Apparently the two men we picked up are the Saturday Night Burglars," Leo told us. "For the past year or so, there have been a series of burglaries at filling stations, stores and bars. They figured that the owners would not deposit their Saturday receipts until Monday, so they would break in on Saturday nights. Lots of times the break-in wouldn't be discovered until Monday morning. The sheriff told me they have confessed, so there won't be a trial. By the way, there's a reward for their capture and conviction and you boys are in line to receive it. I'll let you know."

A reward, I thought. That is something.

There was an account of the burglary and capture in the Fond du Lac paper. It referred to Phil and me as "two minor boys whose identify the police would not reveal at this time."

"If you're under 18, they often don't list names," Dad explained.

"Shucks," I replied. "I thought we would get mentioned for our part in it."

"What you did was important, even though it was a bit dangerous. The key thing is that thanks to you boys, these criminals were captured and won't be breaking into businesses anymore," Dad told me.

Several weeks later, Leo again stopped at our house.

"Next week the sheriff would like you to come to the courthouse. He wants to recognize you and present you with a reward. I'll be glad to drive the family over in my squad car," he told us.

The following week, Phil, Helene and I were excused from school. Leo picked up the family in his squad car, and we all rode to the big, red brick courthouse in Fond du Lac. I sat in the front seat between Leo and Dad. I looked at all the equipment. Leo explained the siren, the spotlight, the two-way radio and the outside rotating lights.

"I don't suppose we can turn on the siren," I said.

Leo laughed. "No, the last time I did it with your family, it caused all sorts of consternation" referring to the time we went Christmas caroling, and Leo thought we were the Huehne kids, coming to cause trouble at Bertha and Rueben's house.

Everyone but Mother laughed when he recalled our adventure last Christmas (told in my first book as "Hardly a Silent Night.")

"We're going to meet in the main courtroom," Leo explained as he parked the squad car next to the sheriff's office.

He led us into the courthouse and up the stairs. The courtroom was a large room with wood paneling and a large, high desk in front.

"The judge usually sits there," Leo explained.

Soon there were a number of officers in uniforms, a photographer and a small group of other people.

Leo introduced us to the sheriff who asked us to sit in the front row.

The sheriff recounted what Phil and I had done and how it resulted in the capture of the Saturday Night Burglars.

"Because of all of the break-ins, the county merchants association had established a reward for the capture and conviction of those committing the burglaries," the sheriff said.

He asked Phil and me to come forward. He then handed each of us an envelope.

"The reward is $500, so each of you gets a check for $250. And on behalf of the sheriff's department, I want to thank you for your part in solving these crimes."

Two hundred and fifty dollars, I thought. I'm rich. I never thought I would have so much money. Why....I began thinking of what I could do with it.

Just then the photographer and reporter from the Fond du Lac newspaper came up. The photographer took several pictures of us with the sheriff and Leo.

"What are you planning to do with your reward money?" the reporter asked us.

"I'll be going to college, so I plan to save it for that," Phil explained.

"And you?" he asked me.

I was ready to start telling him all sorts of things, but then the thought struck me: what if Mother came up with one of her ideas like buying another saw or an accordion or who knows what? Better play it safe.

"I'll probably save it for college too," I hastily explained. Even Mother wouldn't dare to make me spend college money.

COUSIN GEORGE DECIDES TO LEAVE TOWN

"There's a big 'Chalk the Arrow' game tonight," I announced as we finished supper. "Is it OK if I go?" I asked Mother.

"As soon as you finish the dishes," Mother replied. "Just come home when the train gets in."

Life in the Village seemed to be regulated by the arrival of trains. The Village was located on a branch line of the Milwaukee Road. which ran from Milwaukee to Berlin, about twenty miles north of the Village. Actually, the reason there was a Village was because of the railroad. Back in the 1850's, when the railroad was built, there was no town between Waupun and Ripon. Since the old-time steam engines had to take on water every ten miles, and since a farmer with a team of horses or oxen could only make a five-mile round trip in a day, there was a need for a station between the two cities. So the railroad platted a site, and the Village was born.

There were four passenger trains a day in the Village: two southbound and two northbound.

The first train of the day was the southbound train which went to Milwaukee. It arrived at 7:30, and it marked the start of the day for us kids. If we weren't up, Dad would call up the stairs "Time to get up. Didn't you hear the train?"

At 9:30 the northbound train from Milwaukee would arrive. It was the signal for housewives to begin their walk to the downtown area for the day's shopping. Since most people had very small refrigerators (some people even had ice boxes) most housewives would shop every day. Also, the 9:30 train brought the mail from Milwaukee which was the biggest mail delivery of the day. People got their mail at the post office if they lived in town. Only people who lived in the country got their mail delivered.

The passenger train was pulled by a coal-burning engine. Behind the coal car was the mail car where postal clerks sorted the mail from each town. When the train stopped, they would drop off the incoming mail bags and pick up the outgoing mail.

Behind the mail car was the passenger coach. Sometimes on weekends or before holidays, there would be two passenger coaches, but normally there was just one.

The third train of the day headed to Milwaukee and came through the Village at five o'clock. If we were playing at a friend's house, this was the signal to go home for supper since our normal instructions were, "Come home when you hear the train."

The final passenger train of the day came from Milwaukee at eight o'clock. This marked the end of the play day for us kids.

When we heard the train, we would head for the station to watch the train come in. A few passengers would get off, usually someone who had business in Milwaukee and had taken the 7:30 train that morning.

Each evening the routine was the same. We would watch Wes Carley hand the mail bags to the railroad clerk and get the incoming bags in return. He would load them on his hand cart and take it to the post office, a block away. As the train pulled away, we kids would walk home.

"OK, " I assured Mother.

"How do you play Chalk the Arrow? Can I play too?" my sister wanted to know.

"It's a game bigger kids play. We choose up sides. The first side leaves 15 minutes ahead and goes off, making an arrow with chalk to show where they are going. Every time they turn a corner or go somewhere, they make an arrow. Then finally they draw a circle with arrows pointing in all directions and then everyone on the team hides. The other team follows the arrows, crossing each arrow out with chalk—which is why it's called chalk the arrow—and then when they come to circle, they try to find the other team. After they find them, we go back and play it again,"

"Sounds kind of complicated. I don't think I want to play," my sister responded.

Dishes were done, and I walked the two blocks to downtown and crossed the street to the Miller Drug Store, where a dozen or so kids were gathered. We waited a few minutes for a few more to come and then chose up sides.

"OK," said Hale, one of the two captains, " Ann, put your hands behind your back and show a number between one and ten. Dave [the other captain] and I will guess a number, and the closest one gets to go first."

Ann did as instructed, letting several others see the number. Hale picked "2" and Dave picked "8."

"Dave wins," Ann announced. "It was 6."

Good, I thought, we go first since I was on Dave's team.

"OK, 15 minutes head start," said Dave as we left, each team equipped with a piece of chalk.

Our team stopped every twenty feet or so to draw an arrow on the sidewalk showing the direction we were going. We left the business area and started cutting across backyards, drawing arrows as we went. Sometimes the arrows were on trees, or they led over fences.

After about ten minutes, Dave called a halt, drew a circle with arrows pointing in all directions and said "OK, scatter and hide. They have ten minutes to find us all once they get to the circle. Remember, you have to stay within 50 feet of the circle."

We spread out, hiding where we could—behind bushes, under porches and generally out of sight. We soon heard the searching team coming, and we all tried to make ourselves as small as possible.

"Here's the circle," I heard one of the other team members call. The hunting began in earnest. One by one our team was found.

"That's everybody," Dave called. "Our turn to hunt."

We gathered in a circle, closed our eyes and began counting to one hundred as the other team took off, drawing arrows as they went. The game continued, back and forth.

As our team was preparing to hide, we heard the whistle of the train.

"It's eight o'clock," I called. "I have to go home."

"Me, too," came a half dozen other voices.

The Chalk the Arrow game broke up, and we all headed to the train station to watch the train arrive. Wes Carley stood by his cart with two bags of outgoing mail. As the train stopped, Wes handed the bags to the clerk in the postal car and received three bags in return.

Most of us were watching Wes and the mail bags and didn't notice who was getting off the train.

Just as the conductor was calling "All aboard" and picking up the stool which passengers used to get on and off the train, I looked over and gasped.

"Cousin George." I almost shouted.

There, walking toward me, carrying a battered leather suitcase was Cousin George. Well, actually he wasn't my cousin. He was Mother's cousin, or maybe he was her second cousin. I never remembered for sure. He was always called Cousin George by everyone in the family.

Cousin George didn't have a home. He roamed around the country, staying with relatives or friends, working here and there and then moving on.

"How are you doing?" he called when he spotted me. "Think I'll be able to stay at your house for a while?"

"You'll have to ask Mother and Dad," I replied. I knew the answer. Mother would feel sorry for him. "You know," she would say to Dad, "Poor George [it was always 'Poor George' when she talked about him] doesn't have a home of his own and really has no close family either. I think it is our Christian duty to give him a place to stay."

I could hear Dad reply. "Well, I suppose so. But if it turns out like last time, he's going to be gone on the next train."

In some ways, George was a welcome visitor. He was one of the handiest people I knew. He could fix most anything, do all sorts of repairs and build things. (It was Cousin George who built bookcases for us kids since we never did get the bookcases made out of orange crates. which you may remember reading about in *Hardly a Silent Night*.) I began making mental list of what I needed to have done. Maybe some shelves in my room, and he could fix the brakes on my bike. I knew Mother would have lots for him to do. They would be all the things she had been after Dad to get done. Dad didn't like doing these kinds of chores, so he would postpone them as long as possible.

"I thought with the canning season starting, I could get a job there," he told me as we walked from the depot to our house. "They're always short of help, and the foreman told me I could come back any time."

We entered the side door of the house and walked up the five steps leading to the kitchen.

"Cousin George came on the train tonight," I announced as George followed me into the kitchen.

Mother appeared from the living room where she had been listening to the radio.

"Why, George," she said. "it's good to see you. Henry will be so surprised when he gets home from the church council meeting."

Yup, I thought, she said "surprised." She didn't say "pleased."

"I thought I could get a job with the canning factory for the summer," George told Mother. "Herman told me that I could come back any time even if I had to leave rather quickly last year."

I remembered now. One morning I heard George get up early and leave the house. I peeked out the window and saw him walking toward the depot, carrying his suitcase. Mother didn't exactly answer my question when I asked why George had left before the canning season ended.

"Your father thought it would be better if he left now," Mother said, offering no additional details.

"You can sleep in the back room on the couch," Mother told him. "I'll get some bedding and a pillow."

The back room was a small room, located off the dining room. When I had been little, it had been my playroom. Now it had a studio couch, Mother's sewing machine and some large plants. We didn't use the room very much.

I went to bed before Dad came home from the church council meeting. I did hear Dad talking with Mother.

"I hope he doesn't embarrass us again like he did last time," I heard Dad say. "How long is he going to stay?"

"He'll probably be here through the canning season. He'll pay board and room and the extra income will help, especially with Phil going off to college next year "Mother replied. "And he can get all those jobs done around the house which you have been putting off doing."

Mother knew she had Dad there. Mother kept a list of things which needed to be done around the house. On major items such as painting or house repairs, Dad would report to the church council, and the council members would see that things got done.

The list Mother was referring to were small things such as fixing a switch on a lamp, getting the toaster to work properly and a bunch of other minor jobs.

"Well," Dad sighed, "I guess we can give him a chance again. But you tell him that if there's a repeat of last time, he better get his bag packed in a hurry."

"I'm sure he'll be fine. Poor George does need a home. It is our Christian duty to help him," Mother told Dad.

Dad didn't reply, but I could guess what he was thinking. It was hard for a preacher to disagree about having a Christian duty, especially when the person making this point was his wife.

I heard Mother continuing. "I know things will be better than his other visits. He knows you won't put up with the behavior he's shown before."

I heard Dad sigh.

"I certainly hope so," he said.

The next morning George joined us for breakfast.

"Any jobs you need done around the house, Henry?" he asked Dad. "I can get some things done before the canning season starts."

Dad had the list of jobs Mother had been after him to do. After breakfast, George got to work.

"If you need more tools, I know Mr. Liner (our next door neighbor) will be glad to lend you anything you need.," Mother told him. Dad didn't have many tools—a pair of pliers, a hammer, a screwdriver and a saw constituted the contents of his tool box.

"Good idea," George answered, "I remember borrowing tools from him last time I was here."

It was fun to watch George fix things. He seemed to know how everything worked.

"When you're done here, could you take a look at my bike?" I asked. "There's something wrong with the brakes, and I haven't been able to figure it out."

"Sure," George nodded, "no problem."

After lunch, George said he was going to the canning factory to see about a job for the summer.

"You come straight back after that," Mother said in the same tone she would talk to us about being home on time.

"Don't worry—I'll be right back. Besides, I spent my last dollar on train fare to get here," George assured Mother.

True to his word, Cousin George was back in a short time.

"The pea pack is supposed to start next week," George reported at supper that evening. "That means I can start paying board and room."

I thought I saw Dad's face brighten up a bit at the prospect of a little extra income.

The Village, like most of the surrounding towns, had a canning factory. Most of these factories canned peas and sweet corn; although a few of them also canned green beans.

The canning season began in late June. Virtually every high school student who was 16 or older would work at the canning factory. It was a busy place when the canning season was going on. The pea vines would be trucked in from surrounding farms where they would be shelled. Trucks would haul the fresh peas to the canning factory. Here an inspector would take a sample of the peas and test them for tenderness. The more tender the sample the higher price the farmer would receive.

During World War II, there was a serious shortage of labor, so Herman Swenson, the plant foreman(who was a member of the congregation) asked Dad if he would be willing to run the testing office. Dad was glad to do it. He felt it was a patriotic thing to do since most of the canned goods were bought by the government to feed the troops.

"And the extra income will be nice too," Mother noted when Dad told us he was going to be working there during the canning season.

At the end of the season, Herman told him that he wished Dad would work every year.

"Farmers are always complaining that the tester isn't being fair and that maybe some farmers are bribing him to get a higher score. Nobody complained about the results when you were there. They knew a preacher wouldn't take a bribe."

I asked George, "Where are you going to be working?"

"Oh, I'll probably start in the solution room where they mix the salt and sugar," he said. "But Herman said he will probably move me around when things need fixing."

Phil started to laugh.

"What's funny?" Helene wanted to know. Helene was always worried that someone might be laughing at her. "I didn't say a word."

"No, it has nothing to do with you," Phil assured her. " I was just thinking about the time when George was working at the factory during the War, and he brought home the sugar."

I remember that story. Sugar was rationed during the War (as was butter, meat, canned goods and many other things).

One day George had brought home a paper bag full of sugar.

"Here, Minnie," he told Mother, "I thought you could use some extra sugar."

He explained that one of the 100 pound sacks of sugar had broken open and most of it had spilled on the floor.

"We had to throw that away, but there was some left in the bag, so I brought it home," he explained.

"I remember that we had Kool-Aid for the rest of the summer," I said.

"I don't remember that," Helene objected. "How come I didn't get any Kool-Aid?"

"Of course you don't remember," Mother assured her, "you were only a baby at the time."

George got most everything fixed up around the house and then the canning season started. We didn't see much of him. He worked until late in the evening and started early in the morning.

"The busier he is, the better it is for everyone," I heard Dad say to Mother.

"Oh, Henry," Mother answered, "you know George is trying to straighten himself out."

I didn't hear what Dad answered. Maybe he just shook his head and went into his study.

When George got his first pay, he paid Mother for board and room.

"George," I heard her tell him, "let's go down to the bank and open an account for you. That way you won't be tempted."

Tempted, I thought, tempted for what?

"Good idea, Minnie," he answered.

The canning season continued. George worked long hours. Each pay day he would give Mother money for board and room and then the two of them would walk down to the bank. Mother would watch as George deposited the remainder of his pay.

"See, George, you're building up a nice savings there," I heard Mother say to him one day.

Then the pea canning season came to a close. All the seasonal workers took a break until the sweet corn canning would start. George continued to work, converting the factory for canning corn. He worked shorter hours now and ate meals with us.

The break in the canning season also meant that the summer band concerts resumed in the Village park.

The Village merchants knew they had a lot of competition for Saturday night business. Since much of their profits depended upon this trade, they were always thinking of ways to lure farmers to the Village on Saturday nights, so they wouldn't go to nearby cities like Fond du Lac, Ripon or Waupun.

It was Herb Schmuhl, owner of the grocery and dry goods store, who suggested having band concerts on Saturday nights during the summer. Herb had played in the high school band and enjoyed music.

So the Merchants Association made an arrangement with the school to have concerts and the Association agreed to pay Mr. Vogel, the school band director, for rehearsing the band and directing the concerts. As an incentive for the students to perform, each player got a coupon good for a treat at the drug store or the restaurant.

There were two problems to be solved. First, the Village did not have a bandstand in the park by the depot. And second, since virtually all of the band members who were 16 or older worked in the canning factory during the pea harvest, that meant that most of the band members would not be available for half the summer.

Both problems were solved. The canning factory brought in two wagons used in the pea harvest. They were placed side by side and provided a large enough platform for the band. Wes Carley, the

Village maintenance man, strung up lights so the band members could perform.

The other problem was solved by having a split season. There would be concerts in the early part of June until the pea harvest began. Then the canning factory would reclaim its wagons and the students would go to their jobs. When the pea harvest ended in late July or early August, the concerts would resume.

Phil started playing in the band his freshman year, so our family began attending the Saturday night concerts. I guess this convinced Mother that no blatant sin abounded, to entice us children into dens of iniquities, so from then on we could go down town on Saturday nights, band concerts or not.

Mother, Dad, Helene and I planned to go to the concert since Phil was playing in the band.

"Wouldn't you like to come with us?" Mother asked George at supper on Saturday night.

"Well..." George paused, "Ah, maybe I'll come down a little later."

We left for the concert and settled down on a park bench. We were sitting there, enjoying the music, when suddenly Dad jumped up and started walking very fast toward the business section of the Village.

"Where is Daddy going?" Helene asked.

Mother watched him and then replied "I'm not certain," she answered. "Why don't you go and check," she said to me.

I jumped up and headed in the direction Dad had gone. It was only a short distance to the business area of town. Since it was Saturday night, the downtown area was jammed with people. I had lost sight of Dad. I continued walking quickly, keeping my eyes peeled for him.

Then I saw Cousin George heading toward one of the Village's three taverns. Suddenly it dawned on me what Mother and Dad had been discussing about George and why Mother was so insistent about George depositing his pay in the bank.

Just as George was about to enter the bar, Dad appeared. I was now close enough that I could see Dad grab George's arm. As I got closer I heard him say, "I think you should come and join us at the band concert, George."

George was startled. He looked at the bar and then at Dad.

"I think you're right, Henry," he answered, turning and going with Dad back to the Village park.

I followed them, and we all sat on a park bench, listening to the concert. It struck me that George wasn't enjoying the music all that much.

After the concert, we all walked back to our house. Dad kept a watchful eye on George. As we entered the house, Dad said to George, "Let's go to the study for a little talk."

Mother took Helene upstairs to get ready for bed. I noticed that Dad had not fully closed his study door, so I crept into the living room and sat in the chair closest to the door so I could hear what was going on.

"George," I heard Dad saying, "I thought we had an understanding."

Dad was speaking in what Mother called his "preacher" voice.

"But, Henry," George protested, "I was only going to have a beer."

"George, you know very well that if you had one beer you would soon have another and then another. The next thing you would be buying drinks for everyone in the tavern, and after a while you would be wandering up and down the street handing out money to every kid you saw. At least that's what you did last time you were here."

"How do you know all this stuff, Henry?" I heard George ask.

"In a town like this, word gets around pretty quick," Dad answered.

I couldn't hear what George said next, but I heard Dad continue.

"I think it would be best if you figure out where you are going next. I don't think it is a good idea for you to continue to stay here. I'm not going to make you leave right away, but I do want you to decide where you are going to go from here."

I heard Dad get up, so I quickly scurried away so Dad wouldn't know I had been listening.

It was about a week later when George announced that he had heard from Clara, Mother's sister in Omaha.

"Clara says that she thinks I can get a job as the maintenance man with one of the apartment buildings there," he told Mother and Dad. Clara's husband Martin was a janitor at an apartment house and knew about the opening.

"Let me check on train schedules," Dad said as he got up and headed to his study.

Dad loved trains. He had a whole drawer full of railroad timetables in his desk, so he could figure out how to go anywhere in the country. Of course, the only time he took the train was an occasional trip to Milwaukee for a church meeting. But he loved reading the timetables.

He soon returned with an itinerary for George.

"All right," said Mother. "We'll buy a train ticket here. I know Mr. Krueger, the station agent, can take care of that. I'll give you some money for meals, and I'll send the rest of your money to Clara, and she can take care of it for you."

George agreed and a few days later, we all got up early and went to the depot to see George get on the 7:30 train to Milwaukee. From there he would go to Chicago and then take the train to Omaha.

"That turned out better than last time," I heard Dad say to Mother as we walked home. "At least I didn't have to bail him out of jail."

"And the members didn't have anything to talk about this time," Mother agreed.

HELENE LEARNS TO EAT A CREAM PUFF

"Amen," we said in unison as we finished our table prayer before starting supper. It was a special meal tonight: fried rainbow trout, with a fresh lettuce salad and baby creamed carrots, both from Dad's garden. One of Dad's pastor friends was an avid trout fisherman. When he had good luck fishing, he would often bring us some fresh trout.

"Now watch out for the bones," Mother warned us as she passed around the platter of fish.

"It was sure nice of Reverend Adams to share his catch with us," Phil commented as he helped himself to a filet. "Have you ever been trout fishing, Dad?" he asked.

"No," Dad responded, " I don't have the fancy equipment you need for trout fishing. I just stick to the old bamboo pole."

"Well, I'm sure glad Reverend Adams does," Phil answered.

No one had to encourage us to clean our plates tonight, I thought as I took a second helping of the carrots.

As we finished eating, Mother said "And I have a special surprise for dessert tonight—tapioca pudding with fresh strawberries."

We all brightened up. Well, everyone but Phil. Phil would eat the tapioca pudding, but he would pass on the strawberries.

"Why, Phil," Mother would invariably say, "you always used to eat strawberries (or raspberries or pineapple or whatever fruit Mother happened to be serving). How come you don't like them any more?"

Now as long as I could remember, my brother never ate fruit. Oh, he would eat an apple or maybe a banana, but otherwise, he would not eat fruit. Mother would then proceed to tell Phil that when he was a baby he would eat every kind of fruit there was.

"But now you won't eat any of it," Mother told him.

"I just don't like it," Phil answered.

"You just don't know what's good," Mother concluded, always eager to have the last word.

"I have an idea," Dad said, wanting to change the subject. "I think we should go to the State Fair this summer."

The State Fair, I thought. I hadn't been to the State Fair since we had lived in Milwaukee. I remember Mother had gotten all upset because she said I had gotten lost. She would never believe me when I told her I had NOT gotten lost. Everyone else had abandoned me.

Just to set the record straight, here's what actually happened. (Mother has her own version, but what I'm telling is exactly how things happened.)

I was four or five at the time. Our family had gone to the State Fair one Sunday afternoon with the another pastor and his wife, friends of Mother and Dad. Mother hadn't seen them for a long time, so she was busy talking to them and not paying a whole lot of attention to us kids.

When we came to the farm machinery area, I was fascinated with all the tractors. There seemed to be hundreds of them. There were the red Farmall, green John Deere, orange Case, gray Ford Ferguson and the white Oliver tractors. I was having fun crawling up on the seats, pretending to steer and drive them. I decided my favorite were the Case tractors. I liked the orange color. I went back to where they were and climbed on the biggest one.

I was having fun, pretending to drive. Urrrrn, urrrrn, I went, turning the steering wheel back and forth. I was so busy driving, I didn't notice that the rest of the family had left.

I got off the tractor and looked around. No sign of them. Well, I thought, they'll be back, so I climbed up on my favorite Case tractor and started driving away.

As I was turning the steering wheel, a policeman came up to me.

"What's your name, little boy?" he asked. I told him.

"Your parents are looking for you. Why don't you come with me, and I'll take you to them. They reported that you were lost," he told me.

"OK," I agreed. "But I'm not lost. I know where I am."

In a few minutes, I was back with Mother and Dad and the rest.

"Don't you wander off like that again," Mother told me.

"Wander off." I protested, "I stayed right there. You're the ones who wandered off."

Anyway, that's what actually happened.

Meanwhile Dad was talking.

"Since it's Wisconsin's centennial, the State Fair is going to run for the entire month of August, not just the regular ten days," Dad explained. "I think we should pick a date and go to the fair."

I thought Mother would bring up this incident as a reason why we shouldn't go to the fair. Instead, she asked, "Can we afford it?"

Dad pointed out that he was getting some extra income this summer by directing special rehearsals of the Holland men's chorus.

"In that case, I think it is a marvelous idea," she said. "I want to meet Alice in Dairyland."

We had been hearing about Alice in Dairyland. Since Wisconsin was the leading dairy state, someone got the idea that there should be some sort of a dairy queen or princess to promote the industry. Rather than calling her the Cheese Queen or the Cheddar Princess, they decided to call her Alice in Dairyland.

"Why do you want to meet her," we wanted to know.

"Why, haven't you read? Alice in Dairyland is the McGuire girl from Highland."

"Where?" Phil asked.

"Highland," Mother answered in a tone which implied everyone should know where Highland was. "Highland is the town right next to Avoca."

Avoca was Mother's home town, located in the hills of southwest Wisconsin. We would often visit there since that's where Grandpa Olson and many other relatives lived.

"And," Mother continued, "I'm quite certain that her uncle is Patrick McGuire, the mail carrier from Highland, who is a good friend of Alfred's."

Alfred was Mother's oldest brother who was the rural mail carrier in Avoca. Patrick probably was a good friend of Uncle Alfred's since Alfred knew every rural mail carrier in southwest Wisconsin.

"We'll certainly do that," Dad agreed.

"Can Margie come too?" Phil asked. Margie was Phil's girl friend.

"Sure," said Dad. "That would be fine."

Even though it was only June, we began looking forward to our trip to the State Fair in August.

We picked the date we would go. Phil arranged to get the day off from his job at the service station. Dad checked his schedule to be certain there was no council meeting or other church events.

August came and so did the day for our trip to the State Fair. We had been reading all about the fair in the Milwaukee *Journal* and listening to daily reports on WTMJ radio. Mother packed a picnic lunch.

"We'll picnic at noon and eat at the fair in the evening," Dad said. Eating out was always a big treat for us, so that was something else to anticipate.

Phil had driven out to the farm where Margie lived and picked her up. When they got back, we all got into Dad's '47 Chev and left for Milwaukee.

"The State Fair is actually in West Allis, not Milwaukee," Dad explained as we headed south. Phil was driving and Dad was giving directions. Even though we hadn't lived in Milwaukee for many years, Dad knew his way around the city. I had only been to Milwaukee a couple of times since we had moved to the Village, so it was a big deal to visit Wisconsin's largest city.

As we neared the fair grounds, traffic slowed. It seemed as though there were hundreds or maybe thousands of cars, all packed with fair goers and all headed in the same direction.

"Looks as though we picked a popular day to come," said Mother.

"Yes," Dad replied, "I read in the Milwaukee *Journal* that today is 'Madison Day' so I imagine that a lot of people are coming from there."

"Do you suppose the governor will be there?" Phil asked.

"It could very well be," Dad answered. "From what I have been reading, Governor Rennebohm has been to the fair quite often."

"I've never seen a governor," Helene said. "What do they look like?"

We all laughed.

"He looks like most other men," Mother told her. "I've never seen Governor Rennebohm either, so I really don't know exactly what he looks like."

We joined the line of cars edging their way into the fairground. There were parking attendants directing cars.

"Just follow their directions," Dad told Phil.

We came to a booth where attendants were collecting money. Dad reached into his pocket.

"How much?" he asked.

"Fifty cents," came the reply. Dad handed two quarters to Phil who paid the attendant.

We parked the car.

"There's a picnic grounds over there," Dad pointed out. "We'll leave the picnic basket in the car and come back for it at lunch time. Now everybody try to remember where we parked the car."

We joined the lines of people heading toward the entrance gates.

Dad bought the tickets, and we all went in.

"Now stay together. We don't want anyone getting lost," Mother said. Fortunately she didn't mention anything about my last visit to the fair.

There were so many things to see. There was the homemaking building with its exhibits of quilts, canned fruits and vegetables and all sorts of handicrafts. There was the Four-H building with a whole array of projects from farm kids. We paused for a while and watched a young girl demonstrating how to make a cheese cake, using Wisconsin dairy products.

We walked through the farm machinery area, looking at all the latest equipment.

"They call that a combine," Dad explained, pointing to a large piece of equipment. It won't be long and farmers won't be using threshing machines any more."

"Look," said Mother, "there's the dairy building."

"I'm hungry," Helene said. "Can't we have something to eat?"

"Before we left, Dad gave me some money and told me I should buy everyone a treat," Margie said. "Maybe we can get something here."

"I know," I said, "let's have cream puffs."

I had read an article about how cream puffs were a popular treat in the dairy building.

"That sounds good," Phil agreed.

"And after that, let's see if we can find Alice in Dairyland," said Mother.

It wasn't a problem finding the cream puff counter—there was a great big line of people waiting to buy them.

We stood in line, waiting our turn. Helene was the first to get hers. She stood at the side waiting for the rest of us while carefully examining the large pastry filled with whipped cream.

As the rest of us joined her, she took a big bite, squeezing the cream puff. The cream spurted out the front of the cream puff just as two men in suits walked by. The whipped cream spattered the the suit of the man closest to Helene.

"Oh, my cream puff," Helene wailed.

Mother quickly handed her own cream puff to Dad and went over to the man who had been hit with the cream.

"I'm so sorry," she said. "Here, let me help clean you off."

"Never mind," the man said as his companion pulled a handkerchief out of his pocket and said " Here, Governor, use this."

Mother turned white.

"Governor," she stammered, "you're Governor Rennebohm."

"Yes, Ma'am. And who is this?" he asked, pointing to Helene.

Helene had calmed down by now, although she was still holding her empty cream puff.

"I'm Helene" she said.

"Well, Helene, I'm pleased to meet you. I'm Governor Rennebohm and I'd like to show you how to eat a cream puff. Let's see if these nice people will let me cut through the line, so I can buy you a replacement."

Quite a crowd had gathered by this time, including a photographer. The people let the governor go to the counter where he bought a cream puff and brought it back to where we were standing.

"Now," he told Helene, as he knelt down beside her, "here's how you eat a cream puff. You take off the top and dip it into the cream, using it kind of like a spoon. Then when most of the cream is gone, you can eat the rest of the cream puff without the cream spurting out."

Helene nodded and started eating her cream puff.

"Governor, I am terribly sorry about your suit," Mother said.

"Don't worry. From here I'm going to the dairy barn, so I wore my oldest suit today," the governor assured her.

The governor and his aide left, the crowd dispersed, and we finished eating our cream puffs. We all agreed that it was a great treat and we liked the way the governor taught us how to eat the cream puffs.

"Since we're here in the dairy building, let's find Alice in Dairyland," Mother said.

"I saw a sign when we came in that pointed to Alice in Dairyland," I told Mother.

We walked back to the entrance and then followed the sign. As we turned the corner, we all suddenly stopped. There in front of us was this huge animated figure of what had to be Alice in Dairyland. She must have been 15 or 20 feet tall. There she stood, talking with people.

We gingerly approached and the figure spoke

"My, what a nice looking family. How are you folks today?" she said, looking down at us.

"Ask her if she knows Uncle Alfred," I heard Phil whisper to Mother. She gave him a disgusted look.

"We're just fine, "Dad answered.

"Are you enjoying the fair?" she asked Helene.

"It's great. I just had a cream puff." Helene answered. Oops, I thought, wrong question. Now we'll hear all about squirting the governor with whipped cream. But it didn't happen.

"You folks have a great day at the fair and remember to keep eating those wonderful Wisconsin dairy products," she said, turning away and starting to talk with another family.

"Well, that was something," Margie said. "I wonder how they do that."

Helene Learns to Eat a Cream Puff • 71

"There must be a microphone inside and someone controlling it from a booth or something," Phil guessed.

"That was quite an experience," Mother agreed, "but I still want to see the real person."

"There's an information booth over there," Phil pointed out. "They'll probably know when the real Alice will be here."

We walked over to the booth and saw there was a schedule posted:

"Meet Alice in Dairyland in person" it read.

"She should be here in a few minutes," Dad noted, checking his watch.

Mother talked with the woman at the booth and reported, "She will be right over there. We should get in line."

We followed Mother's lead and joined the line. In a few minutes, we heard people saying "Here she comes."

And Alice appeared—a striking young woman, with dark hair wearing a small tiara and a ribbon proclaiming that she was "Alice in Dairyland."

"Oh, we should have brought a camera," Mother exclaimed when she saw people taking pictures.

"I did," I replied, showing Mother my trusty Argus C-3 35 millimeter camera.

"Oh, good. Be sure to get some pictures of her."

I assured Mother I would.

The line moved slowly forward. Finally, we were there.

Alice in Dairyland (whose real name we knew was Margaret McGuire) was a tall (although not nearly as tall as the animated version) attractive brunette.

Mother immediately introduced herself and our family to her and then began quizzing her

"Now is your uncle the mail carrier in Highland?" she asked.

"Yes," Alice replied, "that would be my Uncle Pat."

"I thought so," Mother told her. She went on to explain that her brother Alfred was the rural mail carrier in Avoca and that he knew her uncle through the mail carriers' association.

As they were talking, a man in a suit came up to Alice.

"Excuse me for interrupting," he said to her. "I need to talk with you for a minute."

They stepped aside while we waited.

Alice came back, looked at our family and then asked Mother "Will you folks be here through the afternoon?"

"Yes," Mother answered, "we plan to attend the grandstand show this evening."

"Good," she answered, then turning to Helene, she asked "How would you like to be the junior Alice in Dairyland in the parade today?"

None of us knew what to say.

The man with Alice explained that each afternoon there was a parade through the fairgrounds and that every day a young girl from around the state was was selected to ride on the float with Alice.

"We just got word that the junior princess for today has come down with chicken pox, and we need someone to fill in for her. Would you be willing to do this?" he asked Helene and Mother.

"Can I?" Helene begged, "can I, please?"

Mother paused. She was always pushing her children to do things, but now when it was thrust upon one of them, she didn't know what to say. So she did what she usually did when she didn't know what to do.

"Ask your father," she replied.

No problem here, I thought. Unless it was something bad or expensive, Dad usually would say yes to Helene. Today was no exception.

"Sure, why not? It sounds like fun," Dad answered.

Helene jumped up and down with excitement.

"What do we need to do?" Mother asked the man.

"You need to be at the start of the parade route no later than 3:30," he explained. "We have princess costumes of different sizes, so I'm sure one will fit her."

He pulled a map out of his pocket and gave it to Dad.

"Here's where you should be," pointing on the map. "We'll provide seating for the rest of the family. The parade will end up right where it starts, so you can meet your little princess there," he said, smiling at Helene.

"I'll see you this afternoon," Alice said to Helene. "Now I need to talk with all these people who have been waiting."

We left the dairy building.

"Let's go to the Wisconsin Centennial pavilion," Dad suggested. "After all, that's the main reason why we came."

"This is really interesting," I said as we toured the exhibits. "Did you know that the first European explorer came to Wisconsin in 1639?"

"That was only about twenty years after the Pilgrims landed at Plymouth Rock," Phil pointed out.

When we were done at the Centennial building, Mother said it was lunch time. We walked back to our car, got our picnic basket and went over to the area where there were tables for people who had brought picnics.

"How long until it's time for the parade?" Helene wanted to know as we spread out our lunch.

"It's a few hours yet," Mother told her. "Now you eat a good lunch, so you won't faint when you're in the parade."

Mother always worried about dire events happening to her children. In winter, she always made us bundle up so we wouldn't catch pneumonia. When we went swimming, any time the water was up to our waists, she would call from shore to come back so we wouldn't drown. Mother always called from shore. She never went in the water that I can remember.

"I will," Helene promised, taking a sandwich. We finished lunch, took the picnic basket back to the car and then returned to the fairgrounds.

Goodness, but there were so many things to see. We walked through the the farm equipment area.

"Now don't you get lost here," Mother cautioned me.

"That was years ago," I responded.

There was certainly an array of tractors.

"That's the kind we have" said Margie, pointing to the bright orange Allis Chalmers. Dad just got a new one. He really likes it."

"Look," I said, "there's the Wisconsin Conservation Department exhibit. Let's go there."

It looked like a scene from Northern Wisconsin. There was a lumberjack bunkhouse and a stream with a waterfall. We strolled down the path along the stream.

"Look," cried Helene, "there are fish in the water."

"There sure are," Dad agreed, "I see northern pike and trout."

"Rev. Adams should be here," Phil said, remembering our dinner when we had first discussed going to the fair.

Further down the path we saw cages with fox, mink and badgers.

"So that's what a badger looks like," Margie exclaimed.

We all agreed that this was one of the best exhibits we had seen at the fair.

"We can't lose track of time. We have to be sure to get Helene to the parade," Mother cautioned.

"Anyone want to see the farm animals?" Dad asked.

We said sure and walked to the livestock area. There were barns full of horses, chickens, ducks, geese, pigs, but especially cows.

"Look at them all," Dad said. "That's why they call Wisconsin 'America's Dairyland.'"

There were cows of all kinds: black and white Holsteins, Brown Swiss, gold-colored Guernseys and others I didn't recognize.

"What time is it?" Helene asked as we left the cow barn.

Dad looked at his watch.

"I think maybe we should start heading over to the parade area. We don't want to be late."

Dad checked the map the man had given him and said, "Let's go this way."

Dad was a great map reader, I thought. When we were traveling, he always knew where we were and where we were going.

When we got there, the parade was beginning to assemble.

It didn't look like much of a parade. There was a high school band, busy tuning up, looking hot in their full uniforms. There were some 4-H clubs in green and white tee shirts who looked as though they would be marching. There was a group of horses with riders in cowboy and cowgirl attire. That was about it.

"Look," Helene shouted.

There came this big, horse-drawn float, adorned with a large sign reading

"Alice in Dairyland—Margaret McGuire."

Just then the man who we had met with Alice, came up.

"Good, you're all here. Why don't you and your mother come with me," he said to Helene, "we'll get your princess costume and tell you where to go. The rest of you stay here, and I'll come back and take you to your seats."

We stood in the shade and waited. I noticed there were several more floats lining up.

"It looks like it will be a bigger parade than I thought," I told the family.

In a few minutes, Mother and the man returned.

"Oh you should see her," Mother exclaimed. "She really looks cute."

She turned to me. "Be sure to get pictures."

There was a small set of bleachers near the start of the parade.

"We call this our reviewing stand," He said. "Why don't you sit there" pointing to the top row of the seats. "Since today is Madison Day at the fair, the governor and quite a few state officials will be here in the reviewing stand."

"Oh, dear," Mother said softly, "I hope he got his suit cleaned up."

We all smiled and the man looked at Mother quizzically.

Dad explained what had happened earlier.

"Don't worry. Governor Rennebohm is a good sport, and he probably got a big laugh out of it," he said.

"I certainly hope so," Mother replied.

We climbed to our seats. Soon the reviewing stand was filled.

"I wonder who all these people are?" Mother said to Dad.

"Well, there's the governor, the lieutenant governor, and that" pointing to a man with a big mustache " is Fred Zimmermann. He's been Secretary of State as long as I can remember. He was governor when I moved back to Wisconsin after I got out of the seminary. I suppose the rest are state legislators and other officials."

"Goodness, isn't it something that we're sitting here with all these important people," Mother reflected.

The parade began passing by the reviewing stand. We all stood as a group of American Legion members marched by with the United States and Wisconsin flags. Then came the West Bend High School band, loudly playing "On Wisconsin."

"I wonder how many times 'On Wisconsin' has been played this year," Dad commented as the band marched by. Since the governor stood for 'On Wisconsin,' everyone else in the reviewing stand stood as well.

Then came the 4-H clubs and the other units of the parade.

"Here comes the 'Alice in Dairyland' float," Mother said. "Get your camera ready," she told me.

As the float came by, the governor looked at Helene, smiled and called out, "Hi there, little cream puff girl!"

Helene looked surprised, smiled and waved back. We all laughed, and I got a picture of Helene waving.

We went back to the parade staging area to wait for Helene. The floats returned, and the man helped Helene down. We all said goodbye to him and to Alice.

"Well," said Dad, "I think we should get some supper and then go to the grandstand so we can get good seats for the show tonight."

Eating out for supper at the State Fair! Wow, I thought, that was a treat! But where to go? There must have been a hundred places to eat.

"Oh, look," said Mother, "there's a dining hall run by Epiphany Lutheran Church. I bet that would be good."

"That would be like eating at a church basement potluck," Phil answered. "Besides, I bet Epiphany is Wisconsin Synod." (Our brand of the Lutheranism was the American Lutheran Church and the Wisconsin Synod didn't have anything to do with us.)

"Let's try this," Dad said, pointing to a tent which advertised 20 different kinds of sandwiches. "We can all find something we like there. Remember, fifty cents is the limit for a sandwich and a drink."

"Do we have to have milk to drink?" Helene wanted to know.

"No," Dad answered before Mother could reply. "You can have anything you like."

"I'm going to have Grandpa Graf's Root Beer," I said. That was a root beer only available in Milwaukee, and it was a real treat.

We all decided on which sandwiches we wanted, Dad ordered, paid for everything and when the sandwiches and drinks came, we all sat at a long table under the tent.

We finished eating, stopped at one of the public rest rooms and heeded Mother's admonition to be sure we washed our hands.

We climbed the stairs to the grandstand. Since we were early, we got good seats right in the middle. In front of us was a large stage.

"How come there are bleachers behind the stage?" I asked. It seemed strange that people would sit, looking at the back of the stage.

"They won't be using them tonight," Dad said. He explained that the Green Bay Packers played some of their games here.

"The football field runs between the grandstand and those bleachers," Dad explained.

"But if they're the Green Bay Packers, how come they play here? And why don't they call them the Green Bay-Milwaukee Packers?" I asked.

Dad said that for many years the Packers had played part of their schedule in Milwaukee.

"They may be the Green Bay Packers, but I think they really belong to the entire state of Wisconsin," Dad said.

The grandstand began filling up. A band began a pre-performance concert. The band finished and left the stage. Another, smaller band seated themselves in front of the stage.

As it began to get dark, the stage suddenly blazed with light, a man in formal wear came on stage and the show began.

There were all sorts of acts—singing, dancing, acrobatics, a comedian and what I liked best were the Flying Wenningers. They did all sorts of trapeze acts, flying through the air, letting go of the trapeze and being caught by another member of the troop. Round after round of applause greeted their performance.

Then came the grand finale with all the cast member parading on to the stage, the band struck up "On Wisconsin," and everyone in the grandstand stood and sang and cheered. As we finished, the lights on the stage went off, and the air was filled with fireworks.

I had never seen such a display. Finally, on the ground at the side of the grandstand, the word "Forward" was spelled out as the band again played "On Wisconsin."

We all stood and cheered.

"Well," Dad said, "that was quite a show. Now let's all stay together as we go to the car."

There was a big crowd leaving the grandstand, making its way to the parking lots. We found our car and climbed in.

"You OK to drive?" Dad asked Phil.

"Sure," he responded, "you just tell me where to go."

We inched our way out of the parking lot. It took a while, but we were soon heading north.

"That was quite a day," Dad commented. "You won't forget today, will you, Helene?"

There was no response. Helene was sound asleep.

It was late when we got home. We climbed out of the car. Dad carried Helene inside, and Phil took Margie home. Dad was right, I thought, it was quite a day.

The next day when we got our Milwaukee *Journal*, we were amazed to see a picture of Helene with the governor. "Governor Rennebohm gives a lesson in cream puff eating to a young constituent," the cutline read.

"I'm not a constituent," Helene protested, "I'm a Lutheran."

WHAT WAS IN MR. SCHIFFLER'S BARN

"Martin wants to know if I can stay at his house for a couple of days," I said to Mother.

Martin was a friend of mine, who lived on a farm a mile or so north of the Village. His family belonged to our church, and his parents were about as close of friends as my parents had in the congregation.

"I think that would be OK," Mother answered. "I'll call his mother to see that it's OK with her. When were you thinking of doing this?"

"Oh, maybe next week," I answered. Martin and I hadn't really set a time. I would often play with him out on his farm; although this would be the first time I would stay overnight.

Mother called Martin's mother, and the arrangements were made.

"How would it be if I rode my bike out there? I can carry the stuff I need in my Boy Scout backpack, and that way I'll have my bike there, so Martin and I can go riding," I suggested to Mother.

I was certain that Mother would raise objections as she usually did. I could just hear her come up with things like, "that's a long way—I don't know if you can make it," or "that might be dangerous—what if one of the farmer's bulls got out when you were riding by," or all sorts of other reasons she would come up with.

To my surprise she offered no objections.

"That would be fine," she agreed.

The next week, I took my backpack and rode off on my Schwinn bicycle. It took me only 15 minutes or so of easy pedaling to get there.

Martin and I had a lot of fun together.

"Right now is a slow time for farm work," Martin told me. "The peas are all harvested, and the sweet corn hasn't started yet. The threshing is done for the grain, and it will be a while before it's time for another crop of hay. So there's just the usual milking and feeding the animals."

On a dairy farm, there was work to do seven days a week. Cows had to be milked morning and night. Pigs had to be fed. Eggs had to be gathered. Young livestock had to be fed and watered.

"How come you still have horses?" I asked Martin when we were in the barn. "Your dad has a tractor."

We were standing in front of the stalls holding two big black Belgian horses.

"Dad says it's real handy to have a team of horses. They can haul the stone boat when we pick up rocks in the spring. He says that if we get a bad snow storm and the milk truck can't get through, we can hitch up the horses to the sleigh and take the milk cans in. Actually Dad is just like my Uncle Art. They both grew up using horses, and they just like having a them around. Uncle Art has a pair just like Dad's."

We left the barn and got on our bikes.

"Let's go this way," Martin said, pointing to a small side road.

"Where does it go?" I asked.

"You'll see," Martin answered as we pedaled down the road between a field of corn and the pasture where the herd of black and white Holsteins was grazing. We rode through a small grove of trees and then the road ended in the yard of what looked like an old farm. Martin motioned for us to stop.

"Shhh," he said, putting his finger to his lips.

There was a house, a large barn and a few smaller buildings. We got off our bikes. I followed Martin as he pulled his bike into the grove of trees.

"Who lives here?" I whispered. "It doesn't look like anybody is using the buildings."

"This is the old Schiffler place," Martin answered. "No one had lived here for years until Mr. Schiffler came back last year. Dad has rented the land from him for a long time. Mr. Schiffler seems to be a nice enough guy, but he really keeps to himself. He always seems to be working in his barn, but I don't know why. Let's see if we can peek in the barn."

We sneaked up to the barn on the side opposite the house. We crawled up to the window and were about to peek in when...

"Hey," called a voice, "what do you think you're doing?"

We both stood up.

"Oh, hi, Mr. Schiffler," Martin stammered. "oh, we're just out, kind of exploring around."

"Exploring? Looks as though you're doing some window peeking here." His voice sounded a bit testy.

"Oh, we're just curious. I was just showing my friend around " Martin answered.

"Who's your friend?" Mr. Schiffler asked.

Martin introduced me and added, "His dad is the preacher at the Lutheran church."

Mr. Schiffler paused for a moment.

"So your dad is the preacher at Emanuel," he finally said.

I nodded. There was another pause.

"Say, boys," his tone seemed to grow more friendly. "Why don't you come in the house. I bet you'd like something cold to drink."

"Sure," replied Martin, "we'll get our bikes and be right there."

As Martin and I walked back to where we had parked our bikes, I asked him "What do you make of this?"

"I think he's a pretty nice guy. He just doesn't seem real sociable."

We rode our bikes to his house and laid them on the ground. Mr. Schiffler was at the door.

"Come on in. Never mind the mess. I don't have anything fancy—no Coke or root beer. However, I've got Watkins mix, so I can make you either orange or cherry."

"Great, I love Watkins," I answered.

Watkins products were sold mainly to farmers. The Watkins man would go from farm to farm selling an array of products generally to the farmer's wife. There would be vanilla and spices, a lot of home remedies and my favorite—a flavored syrup you would mix with water and make a wonderful drink. We never had it at home since the Watkins man never seemed to call on people in the Village.

"I'll have cherry," I said.

"Me too," Martin said.

"Sounds good. I'll have the same," Mr. Schiffler said. He took a bottle of the syrup, mixed it with water and then added ice from the refrigerator.

We all sat at the kitchen table.

"So your dad is the preacher at Emanuel," he said again.

I again nodded.

"You know, I really should belong there. That's where I was baptized and confirmed. Maybe I'll have to come one of these days," he said.

"We're open every Sunday," I said. We all smiled.

"When were you a member?" Martin asked.

"It was a long time ago," he replied, "a long time before you two were born."

He grew silent, took a long drink from his glass and looked out the window.

"Tell you what. Finish your drinks and I'll show you what's in the barn so you won't have to go around peeking in the windows."

Martin and I looked at each other, quickly gulped down our drinks and jumped up. We followed Mr. Schiffler out of the kitchen and across the yard. He stopped at the side door of the barn, took a key ring out of his pocket and unlocked the padlock on the door. He opened the door, and switched on the light and motioned for us to follow him into the barn. The stanchions for the cows had all been taken out—probably a long time ago.

We stopped and stared. What in the world!

"Well, boys, what do you think?" Mr. Schiffler asked.

There in front of us was a freshly painted circus wagon. I had seen pictures of circus wagons, but had never seen a real one.

"Where in the world did you get that?" Martin finally managed to ask.

"It's a long story," Mr. Schiffler replied. "Here, let me show it to you and then we'll go back to the house, and I'll tell you the story."

We walked around the wagon, looking at its big wheels and its high driver's seat. We noticed there were railings on each side of the top.

"It's a band wagon," he explained. "It was used in the circus parade. Musicians would store their instruments and music in it while the show moved from city to city. During parades they would sit on top and play."

"Wow! It's really something." said Martin. "This sounds like it's going to be an interesting story."

We left the barn. Mr. Schiffler closed and carefully locked the door. We followed him back to the house. Inside the house he fixed more glasses of Watkins drink and then joined us at the kitchen table.

"Well," he began, "it's a long story. It goes back fifty years. My father had the farm here. It wasn't all that good of a farm. It didn't have as good land as your dad's and uncle's farms have," noting this to Martin, "so he had to work extra hard to try to make a living for us. There was my parents and me. When I said *he* worked hard, I mean we all worked hard.

"Father made me drop out of school after confirmation. I was 15 at the time. He told me that I had enough schooling to be a farmer, and besides I was learning too much English. Everything was pretty much German around here. I was confirmed in German. All the church services were in German, and most of the people my parents associated with were Germans. Of course, I only spoke English in school, but Father thought that was too much.

"Anyway, I stopped going to school and worked on the farm with Father. I didn't much care for farming. I liked taking care of the horses OK, but I sure didn't like the rest of the work—milking the cows, taking care of the pigs, plowing, making hay, fixing fences...there was always plenty to do.

"I did this for a year or so, all the time trying to figure out what I could do to get off the farm and start doing something I liked. I finally came up with a plan.

"I had seen posters around the Village that the Ringling Brothers circus was going to perform in Fond du Lac. I knew the circus had a lot of horses, so I figured that if I got over to Fond du Lac I might be able to get a job with the circus.

"But there were a lot of problems to figure out. I just couldn't go to Father and announce that I was going to join the circus, and would he please give me a ride to Fond du Lac. That wouldn't work.

"It turned out that the day the circus was performing in Fond du Lac, Mother and Father were going to go to a farm auction in Fair water. Father was looking for some more milk cows and figured this would be an opportunity go get some at a good price.

"Now this was in 1898, and the Spanish-American War had started. I decided that when Mother and Father were at the auction, I would leave them a note saying I had taken the train to Milwaukee and was going to join the army.

"That's what I did. Left the note, took a few clothes, a couple of dollars I had saved and walked to Fond du Lac."

"You walked all the way to Fond du Lac," Martin said. "Why that's 20 miles."

"Well, it was quite a hike—took me five hours or so, but I got there without any problem. I found the circus. It turned out that most of the men working with the horses were German, so I got a job right away. I soon found out that the Ringlings were German as well. Their name had been Ruengling when they started their show down in Baraboo some 20 years earlier.

"So I started work right away. I helped drive the horses as they loaded the wagons on the railroad cars, and we took off, headed for Green Bay."

"Wow," I said. "I've read a lot of stories about boys running away to join the circus, but this is the first time I ever knew anyone who actually did it."

Mr. Schiffler smiled and continued his story.

"I got to know Mr. Al Ringling quite well. He saw I was a hard worker and enjoyed working with horses. It wasn't long until he made me a driver which meant that when we had a parade, I would wear a fancy jacket and drive the band wagon at the head of the parade."

"A wagon like the one you have in the barn?" Martin asked.

"The wagon in the barn is the very same one I drove. I'll get to that shortly," he said.

"About a year or so later, I wrote to Mother and Father, telling them I had not joined the army, but was working with a circus. I didn't say which circus or where I was. I wasn't 18 years old yet, and I figured that if Father found out where I was, he might come and bring me back to the farm. I wanted to let Mother know I was OK. You have to remember at that time there were maybe 50 or 100 circuses traveling around the country, so if Father wanted to search for me, it would take some doing.

"Well, the years went by. I kept getting more responsibilities with the show; although I continued driving the wagon because I really enjoyed it. In 1908 I met a wonderful woman. She was a bareback rider in one of the acts. She liked the fact that I was good with horses. It wasn't long until we got married. A couple of years later we had a son. We named him John after my father. I would write to my parents now and then, letting them know how things were going. I never gave them an address, so I really didn't know what was happening with them. Anyway, I let them know they were grandparents and sent them a schedule of where we would be playing. We were back in Wisconsin that summer, and when we pulled into Delevan, there was a letter waiting for me. It was from my father, written in German which was the only language he knew for writing. He was glad to hear about his namesake, but also told me that my mother had passed away the previous year. I felt bad that I didn't know about this, but it was my own fault.

"Well, long about World War I, things started to change. The Ringling Brothers had bought the Barnum and Bailey Circus some years earlier, but had operated it separately. In 1919, a lot happened. Mr. Al Ringling died and then the other brothers decided to merge the two circuses into one, the Ringling Brothers, Barnum and Bailey Circus.

"After the merger, all sorts of things changed. For one thing, we no longer had our winter quarters down in Baraboo. And another thing was that circus parades were ending, so that meant the fancy horse drawn wagons weren't needed any more. We still used a lot of horses to help put up tents and to load railroad cars, so I still had a job. When it came time to head to winter quarters, we took a lot of the old wagons and parked them in the sheds in Baraboo before heading to our new winter quarters, first in Bridgeport, Connecticut, and then to Sarasota, Florida.

"My wife was still performing as a bareback rider Most of my work was now with the performing horses since there weren't parades any more. My wife was teaching our son to be a performer. She said there was no future for him just working with horses. He needed to be a performer.

"It was in 1922 when my son was about your age," he said, pointing to us, "when John was riding with his mother. I don't know what happened, but John slipped off the horse. He got hit on the head by the horse's hoof. We took him to the hospital, but there wasn't much they could do for him. Two days later he died."

We sat there, stunned at his recitation.

"From then on, things started going downhill. I blamed my wife for what happened. She got real depressed. One thing led to another, and one day she packed up her things and left. It was about three years later that I got the papers that she wanted a divorce. There wasn't much I could do, but agree.

"Well, things got worse for me. I started drinking more than I should have. I got a couple of warnings from my boss that I better straighten out. I tried, but I couldn't do it.

"Then one day, the big boss himself, Mr. John Ringling North who had taken over after the last of the brothers died, sent word that I should come to see him in his office The office was located in one of the circus's railroad cars which was parked on a siding along with the other support cars.

"When I got there, he sat me down, stood in front of me and laid down the law like even my father had never done when he was mad at me. I can still hear his words ringing in my ears 'Now look,' he told me, you've been a good employee here. You go way back with the show. You knew all my uncles. If you had been one of our ordinary workers, you would have been out of here long ago. But enough is enough. This is your last chance. You straighten out your life and quit drinking, otherwise you will be out of here.'

"Well, that got my attention as you might guess. The circus was my whole life, and it was my home. I did start getting my life back together. I quit drinking, started going to Alcoholics Anonymous—I found out there was a meeting of them right with the circus—and things got better for me. Even Mr. John Ringling North told me he was glad that I had straightened out my life.

"During this time, my father had died, and I found out that I had inherited the farm. I rented out the land to your dad. I let my cousin live in the house if he would take care of things and keep the buildings repaired; so that all worked out OK.

"I was getting on to retirement age. I thought of staying in Florida where most of the circus people lived. But something kept telling me to come back to Wisconsin where I had grown up. My cousin had died, and the house was vacant.

"So I decided to come back here," he said to Martin "You remember when I came back here."

Martin nodded.

"But what about the wagon?" Martin asked.

"I'll get to that," he answered. "Before I left the circus, I asked Mr. John Ringling North what had happened to the old circus wagons. He said a lot of them had just worn out and had been discarded, but that a few of them were still left at the old winter quarters in Baraboo. I asked if the band wagon I had driven was still there and if so, could I buy it? He said he would check and get back to me.

"A couple of weeks later he told me that the band wagon was still in Baraboo and if I wanted it, I could have it, but I would need to get it out of there. So I arranged to get it trucked up to the farm here, not knowing for sure what I would do with it.

"Once it was here, it sat in the barn for a few months. It brought back a lot of memories for me, most of them bad. But then I got the idea of fixing it up. It would keep me busy and maybe I could have it as sort of a memorial to my son.

"So," he concluded, "that's the story of the wagon."

"You mean, you fixed it up all by yourself?" I asked.

"Pretty much. I took some of the iron work to George Vercke, the Village blacksmith, to have it repaired, but most of the work I did by myself. I had a lot of time, and I knew that wagon pretty doggone well after all the years of driving it."

"What are you going to do with it now?" Martin asked.

"I don't know. I heard that Chappie Fox was talking about starting a circus museum in Baraboo. Maybe I'll see if he wants to have it there. Otherwise, I'll just keep here for the time being. Meanwhile, I would appreciate it if you boys wouldn't talk about it. I don't want a bunch of nosey people poking around here."

We nodded agreement. Mr. Schiffler followed us we left the house and got our bikes.

"You boys come back and see me again. It gets kind of lonely here," he called as we rode away.

Little did he know, or did we know, that we would be back sooner than he thought we would.

COUSIN ESTHER AND THE POOR LITTLE PIGGIES

I was standing in our front hallway, waiting for my friend Rich to deliver the Milwaukee *Journal*. People in the Village got one of two daily newspapers. About half the people got the *Commonwealth-Reporter*, the daily published in the county seat of Fond du Lac some 20 miles from the Village. The paper was cheaper than the *Journal* and had local news. However, subscribers had to go to the post office to pick it up when it arrived each afternoon between four and five. We got the *Journal*. It was delivered to the door each day, and a lot of people liked the convenience plus the *Journal* was a larger paper, had better sports coverage and (which was very important to me) had better comic strips.

We did like getting the Fond du Lac paper to keep up with the local happenings, but as Mother pointed out, we couldn't afford both papers. "Why that would be six cents a day," she explained.

We solved this dilemma by trading papers with our neighbors, the Signers. The Signers lived across the street from us. I shoveled their walk in the winter and mowed their lawn in the summer. I'm not certain how we decided to trade newspapers, but we had been doing it for a long time. I felt that we got the better end of the trade. The Signers were retired, so when they got the Fond du Lac paper, they would sit down and usually finish reading it before supper and by six or six thirty, Mrs. Signer would walk over and leave the paper at our side door.

Our family, on the other hand, would rarely finish reading the paper that quickly. Some times when Mother was busy, it would be three or four days before she would get the papers read, and then I would take quite a bundle of papers to the Signers and leave them on their porch. But the Signers were very patient about this, and the trade worked well.

As I stood looking out the window at the side of the front door, I saw Rich ride his bicycle up the front walk. I opened the door, reached for the paper, said "Hi" to Rich and watched as he wheeled off on his bike.

I took the paper into the living room, sprawled out on my favorite chair and pulled out the "Green Sheet." The *Journal* printed its comics on green paper called the "Green Sheet." Well, it was called the "Green Sheet" by everyone but Grandpa Olson. Grandpa was slightly color blind, and he always referred to it as the "Blue Sheet."

I curled up in the chair and started reading. As I was engrossed in the latest episode of "Mark Trail," I realized that Mother and Dad were talking in Dad's study. I quietly put down the paper and started listening.

They were talking about the letter Dad would be writing in the family Circle Letter. Dad had eight siblings who were spread out over the Midwest. To keep in touch, they, together with my Grandfather Kurtz, circulated a round robin letter among the family members. The Circle Letter made its rounds about every two months and when it came, it meant that Dad would write a letter telling what had gone on in our family since the Circle Letter had made its last visit.

"I suppose you could mention what those two just did," I heard Mother say. I perked up my ears. They were talking about Cousin Esther and me. We were "Those Two" who were always accused of getting in trouble and causing problems.

It's true, when we were little, we did get into trouble when we got together. But that was a long time ago. We were fairly grown up now and didn't cause many problems. Well, maybe the last episode was an exception. I felt it was just an unfortunate accident. Here's what happened.

If you have read *Hardly a Silent Night*, you'll remember that Esther was my favorite cousin. She was about six months older than me, and we had always been best friends. Her mother was Dad's sister and her father was Dad's best friend going back to the time when they were in college and seminary.

Esther and her mother and dad lived in a small town in southwest Wisconsin where her dad was the pastor at the Lutheran church. The town also was my mother's home town, so there were a lot of her family living there as well as Uncle Walter, Aunt Helen and Cousin Esther. I felt I was related to half the people there. Grandpa Olson lived there as did several uncles and aunts, cousins, second cousins, great aunts and uncles and other relatives.

As usual this summer, we went there for part of our vacation. This was a small town, about half the size of the Village where we lived. Early one evening we went to Uncle Alfred and Aunt Ilma's, Mother's brother and sister-in-law. Normally we would have walked the three blocks to their little farm at the edge of town. However, we drove there in Uncle Walter's car since after our visit we were planning to go to the neighboring town where a frozen custard shop had just opened.

"What's frozen custard? " Esther asked me.

"It's like ice cream, only better," I told her, recalling when we lived in Milwaukee. Milwaukee was famous for frozen custard, a rich soft ice cream. It was always a special treat when we got to have a frozen custard cone.

Mother and Dad and Uncle Walter and Aunt Helen were busy visiting with Uncle Alfred and Aunt Ilma. Aunt Ilma had made a pot of coffee, and we could see them sitting around the dining room table, chatting away. Uncle Alfred was a great storyteller, and we would frequently hear laughter coming from the house.

Esther and I were playing outside when we wandered over to fenced yard on the other side of the house. There was a high fence designed to keep Alfred's chickens from escaping. Now, in addition to the chickens, there were two pigs behind the fence.

"I didn't know Alfred raised pigs," Esther said.

"He usually doesn't" I explained, "but one of Uncle Carl's pigs had too many babies, so he told Alfred he could have the two baby pigs if he would bottle feed them."

Uncle Carl was another of my mother's brothers. He had been a bachelor uncle who had stayed with us when we lived in Milwaukee where he had been a school teacher. After we moved from Milwaukee, he got married and had two children. He decided he had enough of teaching and moved back to his home town to take over the family farm.

"What will he do with them then?" Esther wanted to know.

"He'll fatten them up and then butcher them this fall," I replied.

"Butcher them! Oh, the poor little piggies," Esther cried.

"But the ham and bacon will sure be good," I told her.

We went over to the fence, and the two pigs came over, sticking their snouts through the large holes of the chicken wire.

"I bet they're hungry," Esther said.

"Let's go ask Uncle Alfred if we can feed them," I answered.

We went into the house and asked.

"You can give each one an ear of corn," Uncle Alfred said, "but that's all. And don't do anything else," he added remembering some of our earlier escapades.

"OK," we assured him. We left the house and went to the corn crib where the corn was stored.

"Let's find some nice big ears for the piggies," Esther said.

We found two ears and took them over to the fence. The two pigs came running up when they saw we had corn. We pushed the ears through the fence, one for each of the pigs and watched as they noisily gobbled the kernels off the cobs. They soon finished and looked at us, wanting more.

"That's all," I told them. The pigs continued to stand there with their snouts sticking through the openings in the chicken wire, waiting to see if we would bring more food.

We left them standing there and walked over to Uncle Walter's car.

"I sure wish they would hurry up and come," Esther said. "I really am anxious to try frozen custard."

We climbed in the car and sat on the front seat. I was on the passenger side and Esther was in the driver's seat.

"Daddy showed me how to start the car," Esther said. "This is the starter," pointing to a small pedal on the floor. "This is the gas pedal; this is the brake and this. . ." pointing to the other pedal, she paused, "I think it's something called a clutch. I don't know what it does."

We sat for a few minutes.

"I sure wish they would come," I said.

"Me too," Esther agreed.

We continued to sit.

"I got an idea," Esther said. "Why don't I start the car and maybe then they'll stop talking and come out."

I nodded in agreement.

The key was in the ignition. Esther reached her foot forward to the starter pedal and pushed it.

The car was in reverse gear, and as Esther pushed the starter, the car jumped backward. As she pulled off her foot in surprise, she hit the gas pedal, and the car lurched back hitting the fence while two surprised pigs watched in astonishment.

One, two, three fence posts went down before the car stopped. The two pigs, frightened by the noise, leaped over the fallen fence and disappeared just as all the grown ups came rushing out of the house.

"Oh, dear," I heard Mother scream. "Are you two hurt?"

They quickly surrounded the car. Fortunately, neither of us was hurt. The back bumper of the car had knocked down the fence poles, but aside from a scratch or two from the fence wire, the car and the occupants were unscathed.

"What happened to the pigs?" Aunt Ilma asked, once we explained about the car.

Everyone looked around. There was not a pig in sight. Pete Gilbertson (another of Mother's relatives) who lived across the street from Uncle Alfred's had been watching the events from his front porch.

"Ya looking for your pigs, Alfred?" he called.

"Yes," Alfred replied, "did you see where they went?"

"Yup, they headed that way," Pete said, pointing toward the downtown area.

"We better get down there and see if we can find those pigs," Alfred said. "Ilma, you call Max Swensen and tell him to be on the lookout for the pigs." Max was the town marshall.

Dad, Uncle Walter, Esther and I climbed into Alfred's car, and we took off for the business section of Avoca, some four blocks distance.

When we got downtown, which consisted of a block of businesses, the pigs were nowhere in sight.

"Where in the world could they have gone?" Alfred wondered.

About that time Max appeared. Alfred explained what had happened.

"They couldn't have gone too far," said Max. "They've got to be around here somewhere."

"There's one of them," cried Uncle Walter, pointing to the alley between the tavern and the hardware store.

We started running after it, but the pig was faster. He scurried away and disappeared behind the hardware store.

"You two go down this side," Max said to Dad and Uncle Walter. "Alfred and I will go around the other way, and we'll see if we can head it off. You kids stay here and watch for the other pig."

The pig was thoroughly frightened by now. He darted from behind the hardware store and headed toward the railroad depot.

"There it is," called Max. "We'll get him now."

All four men ran toward the depot. By this time, three or four guys who had been in the tavern came out to see what was going on. After all, as one of the men later told Alfred, "it isn't every day that you see two Lutheran preachers chasing a pig on Main Street."

The pig took off across the tracks and headed into the field, leading to the park.

Max stopped. "We'll never find them this way. Those pigs could end up on the highway and cause an accident. I'm going to get the firemen out to help us with the hunt."

He walked to the bank and went inside to use the telephone. Almost immediately the fire siren sounded. Max came out of the bank and walked the half block to the firehouse as men started assembling.

"There's no fire, but we need help in capturing two runaway pigs," he told the volunteer firemen.

"Pigs?" several asked in astonishment. "You called us out to find pigs?"

Max nodded and explained that they might end up being a traffic hazard.

"Let's get going. The last we saw, one pig was heading through the field, toward the park. I'm guessing the other one must be around there as well. I figure if we form a line back of the depot and start walking toward the lake, we should find them."

The men followed instructions. Dad, Uncle Walter and Uncle Alfred joined the line as it moved across the field toward the park by the lake. Esther and I joined the line, walking with the men through the field. No sign of the pigs.

When we got to the park, we stopped. Several men scouted around the park, but reported no pigs.

"Where in the world could they have gone?" Max wondered.

"Maybe they did head for the highway," one of the firemen suggested. "I'll get my car and a couple of us can look for them."

"Good idea," Max responded. Two men walked back downtown.

The rest of us stood around waiting for instructions from Max.

"This probably won't make the pigs appear, but tell you what. If you find the pigs tonight, I'll donate one of them for a pig roast at the firemen's picnic next fall," Alfred announced.

Everyone cheered. . .well, everyone but Cousin Esther.

"The poor piggy," I heard her say.

"Well, we appreciate that, Alfred, but it won't help us find the pigs. And we better find them before we have an accident, and we end up not having a pig roast. Let's go back to town and keep looking," Max told the group.

We all trudged back to town. I was getting tired and hungry, and I didn't care if we ever found those silly pigs.

When we returned to the business area, the men spread out and continued the search. No pigs. The two men in the car returned, reporting there was no sign of the pigs along the highway.

"We checked the ditches along the roadway too," one of them said.

Everyone stood around on Main Street, wondering what to do next.

"Well," Max said, "I think we've spent enough time trying to find these pigs. If anyone catches sight of them, call Alfred."

The men agreed and began walking home.

We climbed into Alfred's car.

"Sure beats all," Alfred said. "Where could those little rascals have gone?"

We drove to Alfred and Ilma's home and parked the car. Alfred went to check the damaged fence.

"Look at this," he called. We ran to where he was. There, sleeping quietly against the chicken coop, were the two little pigs.

"They must have gotten tired and decided to come back home," Esther concluded. "Poor little piggies."

Ilma, Aunt Helen and Mother came out of the house to see what the excitement was all about.

"Thank goodness, you found them," Aunt Ilma said. "I was worried you would spend all night looking for them."

Alfred and Ilma walked to the house. The rest of us climbed in Uncle Walter's car.

"I suppose this means we aren't going to have any frozen custard tonight," Esther said as we drove away.

By way of answer, Uncle Walter pulled the car into the parsonage driveway.

"Guess not," I said to Esther.

I figured we would really be in trouble for knocking down the fence and letting the pigs get away.

However, after we had gone to bed that night, I heard Aunt Helen scolding Uncle Walter.

"You really can't blame those two this time," I heard her say. "After all, if you hadn't shown Esther how to start the car, none of this would have happened."

I didn't hear what Uncle Walter said in reply, but I did hear Aunt Helen say "And another thing, you should never have left the keys in the car. You have got to learn to be more careful."

Poor Uncle Walter, I thought. Esther and I cause the problem, and he gets the blame.

THE GREATEST VILLAGE EVENT EVER

When we got back from vacation, the Village was filled with excitement. The big news was the planned Centennial celebration. It seemed that everyone in town was talking about it.

"Augie said that there are going to be 50 or a 100 exhibits in the park," Phil reported one evening at supper. Augie owned the station where Phil worked and was a member of the businessmen's association, the main sponsor of the celebration.

We soon began hearing about all the other details. Many of the men in town were growing beards to help create an old-time look. Organizations like the Boys Scouts and Girl Scouts planned to have booths. There would be a carnival with all kinds of rides.

Mother was excited when she heard there would be a talent show.

"You know," she said at supper one evening, "I think our family should enter."

Dead silence followed her suggestion.

"What were you thinking of, Minnie?" Dad asked, finally breaking the uncharacteristic quiet which had fallen on our supper.

"Well, I thought maybe we could sing or play instruments or something like that," Mother answered.

"I'll be tied up with the high school band," Phil chimed in. "I won't have time."

"I know I'll have to work at the Boy Scout booth," I said. "I doubt if I'll be able to participate."

Amazingly it was my sister who thought it was a good idea.

"I can sing," she said. "I know all sorts of songs."

Phil and I didn't care who else from the family entered the contest as long as we didn't have to participate.

Mother looked thoughtful.

"Well," she finally said, "I'll look into that and see what the rules are for entering."

We continued to hear more about plans for the event. Every day after work Phil would report on what he had heard at the station.

"There's going to be a steer roast," he said one evening.

"What in the world is that?" Helene wanted to know.

"From what I understand, the firemen are going to dig a big fire pit in the park, and then they'll have a a whole beef steer on a spit with a motor which will keep turning it around. Someone said it would take two or three days to roast the entire steer."

"Then what happens?" Helene asked.

"Well, then they'll make sandwiches out of it and sell them to people, I guess," Phil answered.

Helene pondered this for a time.

"I wonder what it will taste like?" she finally said.

More plans were announced.

"There are going to be a bunch of historical exhibits," I reported one evening. "I was talking to my friend Rich, and he said his dad was going to display his Indian artifacts in one of the store windows downtown."

"They've asked the churches to have exhibits in the store windows too," Dad put in. "Herb Schmuhl said we can have both the grocery and the dry goods windows if the church wants to use them. I thought I would ask the Luther League and the Lutheran Players to come up with exhibits."

The Luther League was the young people's group at the church. The Lutheran Players was the adult social organization at Emanuel. During the 1930's, the University of Wisconsin had encouraged small communities to organize theatrical groups. Since most small towns did not have movie theaters and this was a long time before television, the thought was that theater groups would provide the opportunity for people to perform plays and provide inexpensive entertainment. The Lutheran Players was organized and performed an annual play in the high school gymnasium. Gradually, the Lutheran Players had lost interest in performing plays and sponsored other activities such as an annual strawberry festival.

Other events were announced There would be a street dance on Friday evening. The governor had been invited to speak on the opening day, although it did not look as though he would be able to make it.

"If he comes, maybe he can show everyone how to eat cream puffs," Helene suggested. We all laughed.

Most of of the talk centered around the parade planned for Saturday afternoon, the last day of the celebration.

Phil said the high school band from the Village would lead the parade and that there would be high school bands from all the neighboring communities.

"I heard there will be a bunch of high school bands here," Phil said. "The parade is going to assemble at the athletic field, go up the Back Street and then cut over to Main Street. We'll march all the way through town, and then follow the state highway to the Back Street and then return to the athletic field."

"I wish I could be in the parade," said Helene. "I sure had a lot of fun being in the State Fair parade."

It was then that Mother surprised us by announcing that while Helene wouldn't be in the parade, she would be in the talent contest.

"I talked with Mr. Wesley at his store yesterday. He says there is no age limit, so Helene, how would you like to sing? I can accompany you on the piano."

Helene beamed while Phil and I relaxed. At her age, she loved being the center of attention. We were relieved Mother hadn't insisted on some sort of a family entry.

Later that week I was riding my bike with my friend John. His dad ran the feed mill in the Village and was also the Village president. John mentioned that his dad was in charge of the parade.

"Dad is real pleased about all the bands that will be here. There are going to be a lot of floats as well. Every organization in town is having a float and a lot of the businesses are too," he told me. "Dad says the only trouble is that there aren't any real historic things in the floats."

"What do you mean, *historic*?" I asked.

"Oh, you know, things from the history of Wisconsin or something," John answered.

It was then that I got an idea. I didn't say anything to John, but when I got home I called Martin.

"Martin," I said, when he answered the phone. "I need to talk to you right away. Can I bike out and see you?"

"Sure," he replied. "Just get here before milking time. I have to help Dad."

I told Mother I was going to ride out to Martin's, but I would be back for supper. I left quickly before she could start interrogating me.

I probably set a record for biking to Martin's farm, that is, if anyone kept records.

"What's up?" Martin asked when I got there, slightly out of breath.

"You know Mr. Schiffler's wagon?" I began.

"Couldn't forget that," Martin answered. "Why?"

I explained about the parade and how they were looking for something to do with Wisconsin history.

"Circuses are a big part of Wisconsin history," I told him. "Wouldn't it be great if Mr. Schiffler's wagon could be in the parade?"

Martin nodded and was silent for a few moments.

"You know, with Dad's horses and Uncle Art's team, we could probably do it. Of course, an empty band wagon would look sorta silly," he said.

"What if we got the band from the church picnic, at least the ones who won't be marching with the high school band?" I answered. "There would be a half dozen or so."

"Let's go talk to Dad and see if he would be willing to do this. I know if he will, Uncle Art will have his team there too."

We ran to the barn where Martin's dad was feeding the calves. We breathlessly explained things to him. When we paused for breath, he asked, "What wagon are you talking about?"

"Oops," said Martin, "we forgot to mention about Mr. Schiffler."

"Well," he said after we had told him about how Mr. Schiffler had redone the circus wagon, "so that's what he's been working on. I've seen him coming and going and have wondered what has been keeping him so busy.

The Greatest Village Event Ever • 101

"But if you guys can persuade him to have the wagon in the parade, I'll talk with Art and see about having our teams pull the wagon. We can practice out here."

He stopped.

"I have two questions: first, does Mr. Schiffler want to do this? And second, do the people planning the parade want to have the wagon in it?"

Martin and I looked at each other. We had been so excited about our plans we hadn't thought about these questions.

"Well, we don't have all the details worked out, but we'll get busy and get the answers to your questions," I answered.

"OK, just let me know as soon as possible, so Art and I can begin practicing with the horses."

We left Martin's dad in the barn and went and sat under one of the big elm trees on the front lawn.

"I don't think there will be any problem getting permission to have the wagon in the parade. I know that Mr. Jurgens is looking for something special and an authentic circus wagon would really be special," I said. "I think the hardest part may be getting Mr. Schiffler to go along with it."

"I think you're right," Martin agreed. "Let's go talk with him right now."

We got on our bikes and pedaled down the road to his house. Mr. Schiffler was pushing his hand mower on the front lawn when we got there.

"Hey, boys, good to see you. How about a cold drink? I'm about worn out mowing the lawn. It would sure be nice if someone would invent a power lawn mower," he called as we rode into his yard.

We followed him into his kitchen as he made a pitcher of cherry Watkins drink and then poured three glasses. We went outside and sat on the steps.

"What brings you fellas here?" he asked, wiping the sweat from his forehead with his sleeve. "You wouldn't be looking for a job mowing lawn, would you?"

"Not today," Martin answered. "We've got something important to talk to you about."

Martin proceeded to tell him about the parade being planned in the Village, how we thought it would be great if his wagon could be in it and that his dad and his Uncle Art had teams of horses to pull the wagon.

Mr. Schiffler sat silently as he listened to Martin and continued to sit there, saying nothing after Martin had finished. I considered telling him how great it would be to have his wagon in the parade, but thought the better of it since it was obvious he was thinking it over. Finally he spoke.

"I'm inclined to do it, but let me think about it. One thing I need to know is that they want to have the wagon in the parade. From what you tell me, you haven't talked with anyone about it yet. Is that right?"

"No, we haven't, but we can do that tomorrow," I assured him.

"Tell you what. You come back tomorrow with the OK, and we'll talk about it some more."

"OK," I agreed, " we'll do that."

"Thanks for the drink," Martin said. "See you tomorrow."

We got on our bikes, waved goodbye as Mr. Schiffler went back to his mower, and we rode back to Martin's house.

"Can you come to town tomorrow?" I asked Martin. "We can see John's dad and make the arrangements."

"I think so. I'll ride in after we're done with morning chores," Martin said.

It was about ten o'clock when Martin rode up to our house.

"Let's go down to the feed mill and see if we can talk to Mr. Jurgens," I said to Martin. Mr. Jurgens was the president of the Village and was also in charge of the parade. He operated one of the two feed mills in town where farmers would have grain ground and mixed for their livestock. He was also the father of my friend John who had told me about the parade.

It was only a block and a half to the feed mill, so we walked there. Mr. Jurgens was in his office when we came in.

"Could we talk to you for a few minutes?" I asked.

"Sure, boys, come on in," he said, motioning us into his office. Martin and I both knew him since Martin's dad was a customer , and I frequently went to their house to play with my friend John.

"What can I do for you boys today?" he asked.

We explained about Mr. Schiffler and the circus wagon and how we thought it would be a good addition to the parade.

"That is real interesting. I had heard that Fritz Schiffler had come back to the old farm, but since he isn't raising any livestock, I haven't had any contact with him," Mr. Jurgens said after we told the story. "I think that the wagon would be a great addition to the parade."

We talked some more about the two teams of horses and having a band on the wagon.

"I can see a couple of problem," Martin said. "If we drove the wagon and horses into town from the farm, I think the horses might be tired out before the parade starts. Plus everyone would see it coming into town, and it wouldn't be much of a surprise."

Mr. Jurgens nodded and thought for a moment.

"I think we can solve that problem. I'll talk with Neal Tank. He has that big trailer that he uses to haul his excavating equipment. I think he would be willing to bring it into town. We could do it after dark and store it in the old lumber shed back of the feed mill."

"So, we can tell Mr. Schiffler that it's OK with you to have the wagon in the parade?" I asked.

"Not only is it OK, we will have it at the end, and it will be the highlight of the parade," Mr. Jurgens answered. "You talk with him, and I'll make the arrangements for getting the wagon hauled in. Let me know if you need any help."

Martin and I were smiling as we walked back to my house.

"Wow, that was easy," I said. "He seemed really enthusiastic to do this."

"Yeah, I thought so too," Martin answered. "Let's go back to my house and tell Dad and then go see Mr. Schiffler."

When we got home, I ran into the house and told Mother that Martin and I were going to his house and I would be back later in the afternoon. I left the house quickly before Mother could start asking questions.

When we got to the farm, we found Martin's dad and told him that Mr. Jurgens was excited about having the wagon in the parade.

"I'll talk with Art about his team. You boys go see Mr. Schiffler and check that he's OK with everything."

We jumped on our bikes and rode as fast as we could to Mr. Schiffler's farm. When we rode into the yard, we saw him outside, still mowing his lawn. He stopped when we got there and walked over to us.

"I am thinking about getting a goat," he told us. "It would sure be easier than mowing this lawn. Well, what's up?"

We told him about our conversation with Mr. Jurgens.

"Yup, I knew his father when we used to go to the feed mill," Mr. Schiffler said. "I've been thinking about this, and I have a couple of questions. First, I think we need a band. It would look sorta silly driving an empty wagon. Second, I won't do this unless you boys ride with me."

I spoke up.

"We've thought about the band, and I think we can come up with one."

I explained about the church band, and I was certain that we could get enough players to fill the wagon.

"I would be in the band," I went on, "and Martin could ride with you and help with the horses since he knows the teams."

Mr. Schiffler again looked thoughtful and was silent for a few minutes.

"That would be nice."

He was quiet again and after a few moments said, "Martin, you tell your dad that he should bring the teams over so we can practice. And we need to practice once or twice with the band playing so the horses get used to the music.

"You fellas get busy on lining up things, and I'll finish this lawn mowing. By the way, you don't know anyone who's got a goat for sale, do you?"

We laughed and got on our bikes.

Martin and I didn't see each other for a while. He was busy with farm chores, and in his spare time, working with the horses. Meanwhile, I had talked with Dad about our plan and asked him to help with the band.

"Phil and the other high school students from the church band will be marching in the parade. But I can play on the wagon, and I think we can get the adults to play," I said.

"I'll talk with Herb and the others, and we can practice a few times. I'll see about getting some music. How many will the wagon hold?"

"I think six or seven would be about right," I answered. "Mr. Schiffler says we need to practice a couple of times with the horses so they'll be used to the music."

Things went well. We had our practices, and a couple of days before the parade we all went out to Mr. Schiffler's place. Martin, his dad and Uncle Art were there with the two teams of big Belgian horses. Everyone was amazed at the circus wagon.

"When you talked about a wagon, I thought you might have an old hay wagon or something like that," Herb said. "This is really amazing."

Finally the time had come. The day before the celebration began, the downtown was more active than on the busiest Saturday night. Volunteers were setting up booths for organizations and businesses to display their services or to sell their wares. Other volunteers were building a stage across from the park where events would be held. A big pit had been dug and a motorized rotisserie had been installed where an entire steer would be barbecued. Carnival rides were being assembled on the street where my friend Galen's dad had his business.

Thursday was the start of the three-day celebration. There was a band concert in the park. People milled around visiting the booths and watching the firemen as they prepared to roast the steer. The carnival rides were busy. The beard judging contest was held with winners declared in various categories.

Friday afternoon was filled with activities. The talent contest was held in the afternoon on the big stage. There were all sorts of acts: marimba players, barbershop quartets, accordion performers (but no sign of Phil) and then Herb Schmuhl, the master of ceremonies announced "Our next contestant is little Helene Kurtz who will sing 'Now is the Hour.'"

Helene and Mother walked to the stage. Mother sat down at the piano. There was laughter from the audience as Helene stood and looked up at the microphone which was two or three feet above her head.

When Herb saw this, he quickly walked over, picked up the microphone and held it in front of her so Helene could sing into it.

She probably didn't really need a microphone, I thought as she sang. She really belted out the song. Loud applause filled the air when she finished.

Other acts followed. The judges conferred and handed the results to Herb.

"The judges have made their decisions. There will be third, second and first prizes. The third place prize is five dollars and the winner is. . ." Herb paused for a moment. . ."the third place winner is Helene Kurtz."

There was loud applause. I watched as Helene walked across the platform to collect her prize. Mother beamed from the side.

We didn't even pay any attention to the other prize winners. We all crowded around Helene and Mother, congratulating them.

In the evening, I rode out to Mr. Schiffler's with Neal Tank in his truck. With some difficulty we loaded the wagon using the power winch on the flatbed truck.

"I'll follow you in my pickup and help you unload it," Mr. Schiffler told Mr. Tank.

It was after dark when we drove into town and unloaded the wagon in Mr. Jurgens' shed.

"I'll be here the first thing in the morning to give the wagon a final touch up before the parade," Mr. Schiffler said. "And I might even have a surprise or two."

I hardly slept that night, waiting for the morning to come and the big parade.

When I got up, I had a quick breakfast, told Mother and Dad to watch for me in the parade and then hurried the two blocks to the shed where the wagon was waiting. As I looked down Main Street, I was surprised that people were already starting to gather for the parade.

It's more than two hours until it starts, I thought.

Mr. Schiffler was already in the shed when I arrived. He was busy polishing up the wagon.

"This reminds me of the days when we used to get ready for the circus parade," he said. "Of course, then there would have been 20 or 30 wagons all lined up."

"Well, there may not be 20 or 30 wagons, but this is going to be some parade," I answered. "I hope we get to see everything."

Mr. Schiffler continued working. In a little while, Mr. Jurgens stopped by.

"When the horses get here and you get them hitched up, you can come down to the athletic field," he instructed. He reached into his folder and handed Mr. Schiffler a number.

"Here's your number. Look for your assigned place and wait for the parade to start. If you have any questions, look for me. I'll see you at the athletic field," he concluded as he left.

The musicians began arriving. I introduced them to Mr. Schiffler. Several mentioned that they remembered his parents.

"I remember your mother always brought in her eggs to sell to the store," Herb mentioned.

We heard the sound of trucks outside the shed. I looked out. There was Martin and his dad in their pick up truck with a horse trailer attached. Behind him was Martin's Uncle Art with his pickup and horse trailer.

It took a while to get the horses hitched up to the wagon, but it was finally done.

"The horses should be OK, but just to be on the safe side, Art and I will walk behind the wagon during the parade in case the horses get spooked because of all the people at the parade," Martin's Dad told Mr. Schiffler.

Mr. Schiffler nodded and then motioned for Martin to follow him. They went to the back of the wagon where Mr. Schiffler opened a storage compartment.

"Here, try this on," he said to Martin, handing him a brightly colored jacket.

"What's this?" asked Martin.

"It's a jacket I had made for my son. I've kept it all these years, and when I heard about the parade, I thought it would fit you. I have my old circus jacket too," he said, pulling it from the compartment.

"OK, everyone, let's climb aboard—it's parade time."

"Wait a minute," Herb said. He opened a suitcase he had with him.

"I thought the musicians should have some sort of a uniform. I found these old capes in our storeroom. I haven't the faintest idea where they came from, but they've been sitting around for years."

We put them on over our shoulders and climbed on the wagon. Martin and Mr. Schiffler crawled up on the front seat. Uncle Art opened the doors, and we rolled out of the shed to the Back Street, took a right turn and drove the two blocks to the athletic field. We found our assigned spot. I started looking around as the parade was assembling.

I had never seen so many bands. Our Village high school band would lead the parade. There were bands from all the neighboring towns: Markesan, Green Lake, Rosendale, Ripon, Waupun and even from Goodrich High School in Fond du Lac—three bus loads of band members. There was a cacophony of noise as the bands tuned up and practiced.

There were all sorts of wagons and floats. I could see Mr. Franklin getting his group of students organized. They would be doing square dances on the platform of a truck. He had invited me to be part of the group, but I had explained that I would be doing something else.

I smelled smoke and looked at another float. It was Mr. Vercke, the Village blacksmith. There was a fireplace with a real forge, complete with a bellows operated by his assistant. I learned later that during the parade he made rings out of horseshoe nails and his wife, Myrna, handed them out to little girls along the parade route. Helene was very proud that she had gotten one.

I continued surveying the parade lineup. What in the world was that? It looked like a giant camera. It was! Joan Photo Service from the Village had constructed a large replica of a Kodak folding camera. I could see several of the women who worked there, handing out pictures of the float.

And fire engines! Not only from the Village but from the neighboring communities: Alto, Eldorado, Fairwater and other towns. Hope there won't be any fires today, I thought.

I was looking at all the other floats and marching units when I heard Mr. Jurgens on the loud speaker.

"All right, everyone. If I could have your attention, please. We are about ready to get the parade underway. Please listen carefully. Leo Flannery will lead the way in his police car. The Village high school band will follow. Each unit should follow in sequence. Stay about 25 yards between each unit. The parade will stop every few minutes, so that the bands can perform and so spectators can get a good look of the performing floats like Mr. Franklin's square dancers. We will make a circle of the town and return back here to the athletic field. Be alert and watch. If the parade stops, be sure you stop. OK, Leo—lead the way."

The parade got underway. Since the circus wagon was the last entry. we got to sit and watch the parade pass by. Martin's Dad and Uncle Art stood with their teams, patting them so they wouldn't get impatient.

Finally it was our turn to move out and we began playing. We had three different songs which we repeated throughout the parade: "Barnum and Bailey Favorite," "Hot Time in the Old Town Tonight" and a new piece, "Beautiful Wisconsin." Since the French horn part was basically rhythm, I had all the pieces memorized, so I could watch the crowds as we moved along the parade route.

There were loud cheers when spectators saw the wagon. When the parade stopped, people crowded around the wagon, taking pictures. Martin and Mr. Schiffler were continually waving. The band played and played until my lips were numb.

I had never seen so many people in the Village. There were more people here than there were for the parade at the State Fair, I thought. Later I would hear that the police said there were more than ten thousand people at the parade. For a Village of only 700 people, it was truly an amazing crowd.

We crossed the railroad tracks and headed east to where the state highway curved. The entire route was jammed with spectators. We rode around the curve and then took the Back Street to the athletic field where the parade concluded.

At the athletic field, people crowded around to get a better view of the wagon. Martin and I were constantly being asked by our friends how come we got to ride on the wagon. Other people were asking whose wagon it was and where did it come from.

In the midst of this, a man came up to the wagon and started talking with Mr. Schiffler. I should know him, I knew he wasn't from the Village, but he looked familiar. Then it hit me. It was the man who had been with Governor Rennebohm at the State Fair.

What was he doing here? I heard Mr. Schiffler saying. "I think you should talk to Mr. Jurgens about that. He's in charge of the parade."

I was sitting right behind the driver's seat, so I said, "You probably don't remember me, but our family met you at the State Fair when my little sister got whipped cream all over Governor Rennebohm."

The man looked at me and laughed.

"Yes," he responded, "I could never forget that."

"Do you want me to find Mr. Jurgens for you?" I asked.

'That would be great," he answered.

I put down my horn and got out of the wagon. I knew Mr. Jurgens had to be here somewhere. It took me a while but I finally located him.

I quickly explained that a man from the governor's office was here and wanted to see him.

He hd a puzzled look on his face as he followed me to the wagon.

"Mr. Jurgens, " the man said "I'm Bill Williams, an aide to the governor in charge of Centennial special events."

He went on to say that the Governor's Office was planning to award trophies for the best community events during the Centennial Year.

"Someone from the office is attending every Centennial event in the state. I was very impressed with your entire parade. When I saw this circus wagon at the end, I was awestruck. Wisconsin has had so many circuses start here, but no other town has had a wagon like this—not even Baraboo or Delevan and they're the two biggest circus cities in the state.

"It's going to be a few months until winners are announced since there still are still some celebrations to be held. Then the committee will review all the reports before making the recommendations to the governor. My guess is that you are in line for a trophy."

All of us on the wagon were listening as he spoke.

"Well," said Mr. Jurgens, "I don't know what to say. It would certainly be an honor if our Village would be selected as a trophy winner."

"I'll let you know what happens," Mr. Williams said. "Congratulations on a great parade."

The crowd was leaving the area. The visiting bands had boarded their buses and were returning home. Mr. Schiffler drove the wagon back to the shed, and we all got off. Martin's Dad and Uncle Art unhitched the horses and loaded them in the horse trailers.

"Neal will bring the wagon back on Monday,' Mr. Schiffler told us.

While the parade was over, there were still other events on the schedule such as the fireworks that evening. But as far as I was concerned, the celebration was over.

"It's been quite a day," I said to Martin.

"It certainly has," he agreed as he got into the truck with his dad.

It was in the middle of October when Mr. Jurgens got a letter from the Governor's office. The Village newspaper reproduced the letter which read:

"Congratulations! I am pleased to inform you that your Village has been awarded the Governor's First Place Trophy for the best parade in towns of under 1,000 population.

"The committee thought your community did an outstanding job of organizing and carrying out the parade. The committee especially noted that the inclusion of the restored circus wagon was the highlight of the parade and reflected the importance of the circus in the history of the state."

The letter went on to say that the trophy would be presented later in the fall at a public event in the Village.

The letter was signed
Oscar Rennebohm
Governor

The Halloween Hunt Goes Askew

The Halloween Hunt this year was among the most memorable in Village history.

Before I tell you what happened, I better explain about the Halloween Hunt.

The Hunt was the Village's oldest tradition. It had started early in the Twentieth Century.

When it started, Halloween was a time when there was a lot of vandalism. This was particularly true in rural areas and small towns. Every community had tales about Halloween activities. Some events were minor and humorous, but often antics would get out of hand, and serious problems would occur.

The most common prank was tipping over outhouses. This was before indoor plumbing, and every home, whether in the country or in town, had an outhouse.

"Yup," one of the old timers recounted, "I remember hearing how a bunch of guys decided to go and tip over Old Man Schunk's privy. They snuck up there in the dark and three guys went to push it over. What they didn't know was that Old Man Schunk was sitting in the outhouse, waiting for them. And he had his shotgun loaded with rock salt, ready to shoot. They pushed it over from the back, so he couldn't get out the door. Darned if he didn't fire through one of the holes. Those guys got out of there pretty doggone quick!"

Or there would be the tale of the farmer's buggy hauled to the top of the barn and left there for the farmer to figure out how to get it down.

Some incidents were more serious. One common prank was cow tipping. Cows would settle in for the night in the pasture, carefully lowering themselves to the ground with their feet tucked under them. Cow tipping involved creeping up on the sleeping cow and pushing her over. The cow would be unable to get back on her feet. This meant in the morning, the farmer would need to get help in getting the cows upright.

These and other acts of vandalism had become a serious problem in the Village. That's when the Halloween Hunt got started.

There were various stories on how it began. One was that a wise teacher at the high school had suggested that if the school could keep students occupied on Halloween night, they would have less time and inclination to get involved in pranks. Another story was that the high school principal started it. Still another version was that the Village constable suggested it to the school. However the Halloween Hunt started, it was instantly accepted by students and had developed into an annual event. Originally the Hunt had been just for high school students, but now junior high students were included.

The Hunt went like this. The students were divided into eight teams, four teams of boys and four teams of girls. The Village was divided into four sections. The state highway ran east and west while the railroad tracks ran north and south. This resulted in the Village being divided into four fairly equal sections.

The Hunt would begin at the high school gym. In odd numbered years the boys teams would hide, and the girls teams would hunt. The next year, it would be reversed. Each hiding team was assigned to one of the quadrants a few days before Halloween. This allowed the team captain and co-captain to find a hiding place.

On Halloween night, everyone would meet in the high school gym. The hiding teams would get a half hour's head start. The school bell would ring, and the hunting teams would begin to hunt for those who were hiding. Just before the hunting teams left, each one was assigned to a quadrant.

If the hiding team was discovered, the two teams would return to the school. After one hour, the school bell would ring. If the hiding team had not been found, the team members would come out of their hiding place and return to the school along with the hunting team. There were no prizes—just the bragging rights of either finding the hiding team or escaping detection.

When everyone returned to the gym, there would be a party with refreshments and a dance. By the time things ended, everyone was tired and ready to go home with little thought of pranks or vandalism.

The residents of the Village enjoyed the Halloween Hunt. They viewed it as sort of a community-wide game of Hide and Go Seek. They would watch from their windows as groups would go searching through the neighborhood.

Most people in the Village agreed that this year's Hunt was probably the most memorable. A few of the old-timers disagreed, claiming that the '25 Hunt was the one to remember.

"That was when we got the early snow on Halloween night," Old Man Reuter told the guys at the station. "Heck, it was hardly a hunt at all that year. The boys were hiding, so when the girls came to hunt, they just followed the tracks in the snow. The whole thing was over in ten minutes."

But back to this year. Halloween night came. We all gathered in the high school gym. Mr. Rolfs, the high school principal, was at the front of the gym.

"OK," he announced, "it's just about time for the girls to hide. Girls, you have a half hour for your teams to get to your hiding places. I'll ring school bell, and the boys will begin searching. After one hour, I'll ring the school bell again, and the teams that haven't been found will come back to the gym. Remember, don't leave your hiding place until you've either been found or until you hear the school bell." (The school was located on a hill, and the bell was located high atop the building, so when the bell rang, it could be heard all over town.) "OK, girls, go and hide."

There was a rush up the gym stairs as the girls' teams hurried to get to their hiding places. The boys stood around the gym, speculating where the girls might be hiding. They waited for Mr. Rolfs to tell where the teams would be hunting. This was never announced in advance so the team captains couldn't scout out possible hiding places.

Mr. Rolfs looked at his watch.

"OK, boys. In a few minutes, I'm going to ring the bell. As soon as it starts ringing, you can begin your search. When you hear the bell ring again, come back to the school. Remember, keep searching until you hear the bell, unless you've found your group. But before that, I'm going to give you your assignments. I have put each section of the town on slips of paper. Mr. Wilson has the slips in his hat. Each captain will draw a slip, and then I'll ring the bell."

The captains drew their assignments, and Mr. Rolfs went up the gym stairs to the corner of the first floor where the rope for the school bell hung down. The pealing of the bell sent the teams scurrying up the steps and out the front door of the school. The faculty would spend the hour socializing, waiting for the students to return.

"In the old days, a teacher would go with each group," Mr. Franklin told the others. "Now the students are on their own."

"I'm glad that has changed. I would sure hate to be hiding out in a marsh or a cold barn," said Miss Carnow, the English teacher. She was from Milwaukee and had some reservations about small-town life. She decided to go to her room and correct some papers while they were waiting for students to return.

The other teachers stood around, drinking coffee and talking. The hour passed. No students had returned.

"Looks as though the girls found good hiding places," Mr. Wilson remarked. "No one has come back yet."

Mr. Rolfs looked at his watch. "I have about two minutes before nine. I'll go and get ready to ring the bell."

He walked up the stairs from the gym to where the bell rope hung. He looked at his watch and noted it was exactly nine o'clock. He gave the bell rope a hearty pull and..."What in the world?" he exclaimed. Instead of the bell pealing, the rope came sliding down from the ceiling and was now piled up in front of him. He ran down the stairs to the gym.

"Find Walt," he yelled, "the bell rope broke."

Walt was the school janitor. But he was much more than that. As far as the school and the Village were concerned, he was pretty much Mr. Indispensable. During the years of World War II, he had served as the high school coach. He would drive a school bus if the regular driver wasn't available and would generally drive the bus to away athletic events. If a referee failed to show up for a game, he would be pressed into service.

He would even take over a class if a teacher got sick or had to leave unexpectedly. All that plus keeping the school building up and running. During the winter he would open the school gym on Saturdays so kids could come in and shoot baskets. Whenever there was any sort of problem at school, the usual reaction was, "Get Walt."

It just wasn't at the school where he was active. He was also the assistant chief of the volunteer fire department. In the winter he would help flood the park so kids would have a skating rink. In the summer, if the businessmen's association decided to sponsor fireworks on the Fourth of July, Walt would be the one to set them off. Not much happened in the Village that didn't involve Walt.

One of the teachers headed to the boiler room where Walt would usually be found.

"Wait a minute," called Mr. Franklin. "Walt said he was going home and would be back later to lock up."

"Call his house," Mr. Rolfs said, "we need to ring the bell to get the kids back. No one is going to come out of hiding, or quit hunting until the bell sounds."

Mr. Wilson went to the office to call Walt.

"Let me go up in the belfry to see if I can ring the bell without the rope," said Mr. Thomas, the coach.

"Good idea," said Mr. Rolfs, "but be careful. I don't know how good the ladder is up there."

Mr. Thamos and Mr. Franklin climbed the stairs to the third floor and found the ladder which led to the trap door. This was the access to the belfry.

"Should I come with you?" Mr. Franklin asked the coach.

"Stay here and hold the ladder. I'm guessing there probably isn't a lot of room up there."

He climbed up the ladder and disappeared through the trap door. Mr. Franklin waited. Suddenly he heard a crash and the sound of breaking wood.

Mr. Franklin quickly climbed up the ladder.

"What happened, Coach?" he asked, calling to him through the trap door.

"The ladder up here collapsed and I'm trapped. I can't move, and I can't see a thing. I'm afraid to try moving too much because I can't see anything and I might fall. Get some help and some light," Coach answered.

Mr. Franklin hurried down the stairs to the office where Mr. Rolfs was standing. He reported what had happened. Mr. Wilson had just said that there was no answer at Walt's house. Just then Miss Carnow emerged from her room.

"Why hasn't the bell rung? It's been an hour. We can't leave the students out there," she said.

Mr. Rolfs turned and went into the office.

"First, I'm going to call the fire department to see if they can get Coach out of the tower. Then," turning to Mr. Wilson, " I want you to call Reverend Kurtz and ask him to ring the Lutheran church bell. Maybe when the kids hear that, they'll come back to the school."

Mr. Rolfs picked up the phone. When the operator answered, he said he wanted the fire department called but explained there was no fire. Moments later the fire whistle sounded to summon the volunteer firemen to the station.

Meanwhile, Mr. Wilson called the Lutheran parsonage. Dad told us later what had happened.

"I was certainly surprised when I got Mr. Wilson's call, asking me to have the church bell rung. I told him that I would call Ornie and see if he could do it," Dad told us.

Ornie was the church's janitor. He lived across the street from the parsonage. Fortunately, Dad got hold of Ornie before he went to answer the fire alarm. Ornie was a volunteer fireman and was just getting ready to go to the fire station.

"I'll ring the bell first," he told Dad, "Then I'll find out if they need me at the fire."

A few minutes later, the church bell started ringing. Now the only time the church bell at Emanuel would ring other than before services was when someone died. The congregation had the custom that at the death of a member, the church bell would ring. This would be followed by tolling the bell, with a stroke for each year of the deceased's age. Usually when this happened, people would figure out who had died, but if they didn't, they would call the parsonage.

But tonight the bell kept ringing. There was no tolling.

Soon the parsonage phone started to ring.

"Did someone die?" the caller would ask.

Each time Mother would patiently explain the situation.

Meanwhile, downtown at the fire station, Chief Mason had received word why the department was being called.

"We'll need ladders, portable lights and our axes. Probably a half dozen men can handle things. Why don't you guys come (pointing to the first arrivals) and the rest can go back home. I don't think we'll need any more. Let's go," he said.

The men climbed aboard the fire truck and took off for the school, some four blocks away.

Mr. Rolfs met them at the door of the school, explained the situation, and the firemen carried their equipment up the stairs where Mr. Franklin was waiting at the bottom of the ladder.

"Don't worry, Coach," Chief Mason called, "we'll have you out in no time."

Walt was one of the firemen who had responded to the call, so he volunteered to go up to see what the situation was with Coach.

Walt took one of the portable lights with him as he crawled up the ladder.

"I think we're going to need a saw to get Coach out," he called. "Mr. Franklin, could you go down to the boiler room and get a saw from my work bench?"

Meanwhile, both the hiding and hunting groups had heard the church bell ringing.

"It doesn't sound like the school bell," whispered Patricia VanderHeoevel, one of the hiding group captains "You don't suppose the boys are trying to trick us so that we come out before the time is up."

"Does anyone know what time it is?" asked Angie Bruggemann, her co-captain. "Who's got a watch?"

No one had a watch, but several guessed the hour must be up.

"Let's go back," one of the girls said, "I have to go to the bathroom."

Meanwhile the boys were wondering why the bell was ringing.

"That's the Lutheran church bell, isn't it?" Ron Bumpers, our team's captain asked me.

The Halloween Hunt Goes Askew • 119

"Sure sounds like it," I agreed.

"We've looked all over. I don't think we'll find them," Ron said. "Besides, I'm certain the hour is up."

One by one the teams straggled back to the school, certain that the time had expired. No hiding teams had been found.

As the students came to the school, they were surprised to see the fire truck parked in front of the building, lights flashing. A group of adults watched what was going on. A couple of firemen kept them out of the school. The firemen explained what had happened.

The firemen finally allowed the students to enter and told them to report to the gym.

Meanwhile, up in the belfry, things were not going well. Mr. Franklin had brought the saw to Walt. Walt called down to Ed, one of the firemen who was standing at the bottom of the ladder with Mr. Franklin.

"Ed, bring another light and come up here. This looks complicated."

Ed got another light and crawled up the ladder. About that time Mr. Rolfs came to see what was taking so long.

"Are you OK, Coach?" he called up.

"I'm OK, but it's not exactly how I planned to spend Halloween night," came his answer.

"All the students are back, so we don't have to worry about ringing the bell tonight. We can probably get along without it for a couple of days, so let's just get Mr. Thomas down from there," Mr. Rolfs directed.

"Well, I wasn't planning to replace the rope tonight anyway," Walt said as he worked to saw the boards which were holding Coach captive.

Just then, Miss Carnow came running up the stairs.

"Mr. Rolfs," she panted, out of breath from running up all the stairs from the gymnasium. "Patricia VandenHoevel's team hasn't come back. You've got to do something. Those poor girls might catch pneumonia out there."

Mr. Rolfs paused. What more could go wrong? he thought.

"Excuse me, Mr. Rolfs, but I have a suggestion."

Mr. Rolfs looked at the fireman who had just spoken.

"I'm looking for all the help I can get, J.B." he said

"Let's get my truck. It's got the loudspeaker on it. We can drive through the quadrant where they're hiding and tell them to come back to the school."

J.B. was the telephone company's maintenance man. He also used the telephone truck for Village events and if an emergency developed.

"Good idea, "Mr. Rolfs answered. "Get your truck, and I'll meet you in front of the school." J.B. left and Mr. Rolfs turned to Miss Carnow.

"Miss Carnow, do you remember which quadrant Patricia's team is hiding in?"

"I think you said they would be in the northwest section," she answered.

J.B. lived a couple of blocks from the school. By the time Mr. Rolfs got his coat on and went outside, J.B. was waiting for him.

The northwest quadrant was the largest of the four quadrants. It ran about ten blocks east and west and four to five blocks north and south. It included the canning factory, some open fields and a marshy area.

J.B. handed the microphone to Mr. Rolfs.

"Push the button and speak into it," he instructed. "Tell me where to drive."

"Let's start by the tracks and move west paralleling Main Street," Mr. Rolfs suggested.

As they began slowly driving west, Mr. Rolfs began announcing, "Patricia, this is Mr. Rolfs. The hunt is over. Please return your team to the school."

"See anyone?" he asked J.B.

"Nope. I'll keep driving and you keep talking."

They slowly moved down the street until it ended.

"Take the street to the canning factory," Mr. Rolfs suggested. He kept repeating the announcement.

J.B.'s truck had a searchlight on it and he began moving it back and forth as Mr. Rolfs continued announcing. They could see lights going on in houses as people who had gone to bed early

The Halloween Hunt Goes Askew • 121

were awakened by the announcements and were looking out their windows to see what was happening.

It was at the edge of the canning factory grounds when J.B. halted his truck.

"There they are," he said as the group of girls came walking down the street.

Mr. Rolfs got out of the truck and walked to the girls.

"The rope to the school bell broke, so we couldn't ring the school bell," he explained. "That's why we had them ring the Lutheran Church bell."

"Well, we heard the church bell, but since your instructions were to come back when we heard the school bell, we just stayed where we were," Patricia explained. "No one had a watch, so we didn't know that the hour was up."

"That's fine," Mr. Rolfs assured her. "You followed instructions and there's no problem. We were just concerned that you were all OK. Let's go back to the school for the Halloween party."

The fire truck was pulling away from the school as J.B. and Mr. Rolfs returned.

"Look as though everything is OK," J.B. said. "I"ll take the truck and go home."

"Thanks for your help, J.B." said Mr. Rolfs as he got out of the truck.

In a few minutes Patricia and her team arrived at the school, much to Miss Carnow's relief.

"I was so worried about all of you," she told Patricia.

Coach Thomas was in the gym with the other teachers.

"No worse for wear," he told Mr. Rolfs, "but next time I don't think I'll be so quick to volunteer."

"It's certainly has been a Halloween Hunt we won't forget," agreed Mr. Rolfs.

WHAT HAPPENED TO THE HUEHNE KIDS

We had finished our table prayer at supper, and as we were passing the food around, Dad began the conversation with "Anything new at school today?"

"Bub Huehne got sent to the principal's office," I answered.

"That's hardly news," Phil said. "It happens every week."

Phil was right. Bub Huehne was always getting sent to the principal's office. There weren't many things which Mr. Franklin couldn't handle by himself, but Bub Huehne was the exception.

I better explain. There were three Huehne kids. Beulah was the oldest, several years older than Bub who was in my class. Beulah was tough. She was better in sports than most of the boys, No one could push her around. Bub, his real name was Robert, but only teachers and the principal called him that. Bub was mean, picking on younger kids and not paying attention in class. Guerdon—his name was not Gordon, he would tell people, it was Guerdon—was a few years younger. Guerdon, who if you called him "Gordon" would immediately correct you and usually include a few choice words of profanity. The three of them always hung out together. People were always accusing them of causing trouble like breaking windows and things like that; although, they were rarely caught doing things.

Mr. Franklin was our teacher. He was a great teacher who went out of his way to help kids. Yet he never seemed to be able to get through to Bub. Almost every week Mr. Franklin would reach the point of exasperation and end up sending Bub to see Mr. Rolfs, the principal. Mr. Rolfs would talk with Bub who would sit there, seemingly not paying attention. Mr. Rolfs would then call Bub's parents, or at least try to call them to have them come to the school. Usually they wouldn't answer the phone, and when they did, Bub's mother would always have an excuse why her husband and she couldn't come to the school.

Mr. Huehne didn't have a regular job. He would work in the canning factory during the summer, do odd jobs around town and whatever other work he could find. He also spent a lot of time hanging around the Village's three taverns.

"So what happened with Bub this time?" Phil asked.

"Nothing much. He came back from the principal's office, took his seat and sat there. Those Huehne kids are sure a bunch of losers," I responded.

"You know," Dad interrupted, "maybe there are some things we don't know about."

"What do you mean?" I wanted to know.

"Well," Dad explained, "I've been thinking about them."

That's a surprise, I thought. Why would Dad be thinking about the Huehne kids?

"They really should be attending Sunday School and confirmation class here," Dad went on.

"I didn't know they were Lutheran," Phil said. "I didn't think they belonged to any church."

"I was going through the church records, and I noticed that both Beulah and Robert were baptized here," Dad said.

"What about Guerdon? Wasn't he baptized?" Helene wanted to know.

"There's no record on Guerdon. Maybe he wasn't baptized. I don't know," Dad told her. "Anyway, the other day I went to call on them to see if I could get the kids to come to Sunday School and confirmation class."

"I didn't know that," Mother broke in. "What happened?"

"Nothing," Dad replied. "I knocked and I saw Mrs. Huehne peek through the corner of the curtain. I knocked again, but she never answered the door. I felt like she was scared to come to the door."

We all agreed that it was a pretty sad situation, and since no one had anything else to add, we began talking about other things.

A week or so later at supper, Dad announced that he was going to meet with Mr. Rolfs to discuss the Huehne family.

"Are you coming to school?" Helene wanted to know.

"No, Mr. Rolfs thought it would be better if he came here," Dad replied. "He's going to stop over tomorrow night."

Nothing more was said. We knew better than to ask questions when it involved Dad's work as a pastor. We also knew that we didn't discuss things like this with anyone outside of the family.

"A lot of what Dad does with members is confidential, so even if we know about it, we should never mention it to anyone," Mother had warned us on more than one occasion.

The next evening Mr. Rolfs came to Dad's study. The study was Dad's office where he did his church work such as meeting with parishioners, working on sermons and doing all of the other things involved with a pastor's duties. The study was a separate room and had its own entrance so people did not have to go through the parsonage to see Dad.

The next evening at supper we waited to see if Dad had anything to report on his meeting with Mr. Rolfs. He had a brief comment.

"Mr. Rolfs was interested in what I had to say. He too has been concerned about the Huehnes and really doesn't know what to do. He said he was going to give it some thought and would get back to me."

About a week later at supper, Dad mentioned, "I had a call from Mr. Rolfs today. He wants me to come to a meeting at the school. He's going to have Mr. Franklin, Miss Robin and Leo Flannery, and he thought I should come as well."

Having Mr. Franklin there would make sense since he was Bub's teacher. And Miss Robin was Guerdon's teacher.

"But why Mr. Flannery?" I asked. Leo Flannery was the deputy sheriff who lived in the Village. "Are they in trouble with the law?"

"No, nothing specific, but there have been a number of complaints about the Huehne kids. You remember what happened last Christmas time."

Everyone but Mother started to laugh. That was when our family had gone Christmas caroling the week after Christmas, and the people where we were caroling had thought we were the Huehne kids and had called Leo.

"Mr. Rolfs thought it would be helpful to have him there along with the teachers. Since I'm the one who initiated the subject, Mr. Rolfs asked me to be there as well," Dad explained.

Nothing more was said. We kids were anxious to know what would happen, but we also realized that Dad would probably not be able to tell us any details.

The meeting was held at the school one evening in the following week. At supper the next evening, Dad only mentioned that it had been a good meeting, but that he really couldn't say anything at this time.

One morning at school a couple of weeks later, we saw a stranger enter the building. None of us recognized the woman.

"Who's that?" I asked my friend Ron. Ron's dad was on the school board, so I thought he might know.

"Don't know," said Ron, shaking his head. "I don't recognize her."

Mr. Franklin had just started our reading class when there was a knock on the door of the classroom. We all peered at the door as Mr. Franklin went to answer it.

"It's Mr. Rolfs," Norm whispered to me. "I wonder why he's here?"

Mr. Franklin turned to the class.

"I need to talk with Mr. Rolfs for a few minutes, so finish reading the chapter. I'll be right outside the door, so don't get too rambunctious," he said with a smile.

The door closed. A few minutes later, it opened and Mr. Franklin reentered the room.

"Robert," he said to Bub Huehne, "Mr. Rolfs would like to talk with you."

What did he do now? was the thought going through the minds of everyone in the class. Usually Bub was sent to the office after he had caused trouble in class or on the playground.

"Don't worry, Robert. You're not in trouble," he said to a relieved-looking Bub. "Just go to the office."

Class resumed. Bub was gone for about a half hour, and when he returned, we were all itching to know what had happened. He said nothing. Mr. Franklin said nothing. The rest of us sat at our desks wondering what was going on.

I mentioned the incident at the supper table. Phil reported that Beulah had also been excused from a class to go to the office, and Helene said she thought she had seen Guerdon in the hall later in the morning.

Dad said nothing and after some speculation on our part, we finished supper talking about other topics.

A couple of weeks later, another stranger came to school. She was carrying what looked like some sort of a suitcase.

"I think I've seen her before," I said to Norm, "but I sure can't remember."

"That's Miss Threweg, the county nurse," said Alice. "Remember, she was the one who came and told us why we had to take goiter pills."

A number of years ago, researchers at the University of Wisconsin had discovered that the reason so many Midwestern school children had enlarged thyroid glands or goiters was a lack of iodine in their diet. Eventually this problem would be cured by introducing iodized salt, and the goiter pills would be discontinued.

"Maybe she's here to tell us about something else," said Allen who was standing nearby. "That way we'll get out of class."

No such luck. Class started without any word from Mr. Franklin about being dismissed from class to hear Miss Threweg. A short time later, there was a knock on the door. Mr. Franklin answered it, then stepped back into the room and said, "Robert, will you go to the office, please?"

Bub got up and left the room. We resumed our reading lesson, continuing to wonder what was going on with Bub and the other Huehne kids.

At supper I reported what had happened. Neither Phil nor Helene mentioned anything about Beulah or Guerdon. Dad again said nothing.

A week or two later, there was another visitor at the school. We saw her park her car in front of the school. We watched through the classroom window.

"Do you know who that is?" I asked Alice. "She's driving a Fond du Lac County car."

Alice's Dad was Leo Flannery, the deputy sheriff. Since he worked for the county, I thought Alice might know.

"No, I don't recognize her. I wonder if Bub will get called to the office again?" she answered.

Class started. Nothing happened in the morning. It was just after lunch when Mr. Rolfs came to the door and asked Bub to come to the office with him.

"This is very strange," I whispered to Norm.

"I wonder what's going on," he agreed.

At supper, we all had the same report: all three Huehne kids had been called out of class that day. Again Dad said nothing.

It was about a week or so later at supper that Dad said Mr. Rolfs had called and asked him to come to a meeting at the school the next evening.

"I know you are all interested in what is going on," he told Phil, Helene and me, "but I think you understand why I can't tell you anything at this time. I will say that I am hoping that some positive things will be happening soon."

We had all sorts of questions we wanted to ask Dad, but we knew that we had to wait until he could tell us more.

Several days later the Fond du Lac County car was again parked in front of the school. We were very surprised when we looked out of the window and saw Bub and his mother get into the car with the woman who had been at the school before.

When class started, Mr. Franklin had an announcement.

"I know that many of you have been wondering what has been going on lately with Robert. As you probably noticed, Robert isn't here today, and I need to tell you that I owe Robert an apology."

We looked at one another. Mr. Franklin owed Bub an apology? I thought it was more likely the other way around for all the times Mr. Franklin had to send him to the office.

"Yes," Mr. Franklin continued, "I owe him an apology, and I plan to do so the first chance I have."

Mr. Franklin then proceeded to tell the class that he, Mr. Rolfs and several others had been meeting to talk about Bub's behavior. He didn't mention Dad or Deputy Flannery.

"We talked with the county nurse and the county social worker. It was the county nurse who noticed that Robert seemed to have hearing problems. She came and tested him and discovered that he was quite hard of hearing. He can hear OK when you talk directly with him, but not when it's a situation like a class setting. The social worker said that probably accounted for his behavior problems.

"Now I have to admit I should have been smart enough to figure this out, but I didn't. That's why I owe Robert an apology. I believe his behavior problem is class is largely due to the fact he isn't able to hear everything.

"Today Robert and his mother went to Fond du Lac with the county nurse. He's going to be fitted with a hearing aid. The nurse feels that if he has one, he'll participate in class discussion more and his behavior should improve as well," said Mr. Franklin.

"Now," he continued, "when Robert comes back to our class, I don't want anyone here to make fun of him, to say things to him about his hearing aid or anything else. Having a hearing aid is no different than wearing glasses."

"And one more thing," Mr. Franklin's voice grew unusually stern, "if I catch anyone making fun of him or teasing him, I guarantee that you are going to be in bigger trouble than you can imagine."

We all nodded. No one wanted to take this kind of a chance.

At supper that evening, Dad smiled when I reported that Bub was going to get a hearing aid.

"I think we have made a lot of progress in helping the Huehne children," Dad said. There are some other things happening which I can't tell you about now, but I am hoping there will be good news sometime soon."

We wondered what Dad meant, but again we knew we couldn't ask.

The next day Bub was back in class. We noticed he had something on the back of each ear. None of us said a word. Bub didn't say anything either, but we noticed he did seem to pay more attention than usual. As we left for recess, I noticed that Mr. Franklin motioned for Bub to stay, and I saw them talking as I walked out the door of the classroom.

After recess, Mr. Franklin had an announcement.

"I talked with Robert, and he wants to say something to the class. Robert."

Bub stood up at his desk.

"I wanted you to know that a couple of weeks ago when the county nurse was here, she checked my hearing and found out I had a problem hearing things, especially in class. So yesterday, Ma and I went with the county nurse to Fond du Lac, and I got these things for my ears. The county nurse said it was like getting glasses, only they're for the ears, not the eyes. I guess that's all I gotta say," he said, looking at Mr. Franklin.

"Thank you for telling us about this, Robert. I hope you will be able to hear better. It may take you a while to get used to it, just like it took me a while to get used to wearing glasses," Mr. Franklin told him.

At supper I reported what had happened at class. Dad mentioned that he had another meeting coming up, and that was all that was said.

Dad went to the meeting, but didn't say anything to us about what took place. We wondered, but said nothing, not to our friends or at home. We figured when Dad could tell us something, he would. Otherwise, it was better not to ask questions.

Weeks went by. Bub was doing better in class. He had not been sent to the principal's office since he had gotten his hearing aids.

At supper one evening Dad said Mr. Rolfs had called and asked him to come to the school the next evening.

"I hope we can get things resolved pretty soon," he said "I seem to be spending a lot of time on the Huehnes, and they're not even members. But it's for a worthwhile cause."

We continued to wonder what was going on. Dad went to the meeting, but again, there was no report.

It was a week or so later at supper, right after our table prayer that Dad had an announcement.

"I know you all have been wondering about all the meetings I have been attending about the Huehne kids. You know about Bub and his hearing aid. From what I understand, that has been real helpful. But a lot of other things have taken place, and I thought you would like to know," Dad said.

What he told us made us feel bad about how we had viewed the three Huehne children.

"You all know how tough Beulah is and how the three of them always go around together. Mr. Rolfs and Mr. Flannery were the ones who began to put the pieces together.

"They called in the county social worker and through her interviews, she found that there were all sorts of problems at the Huehne home."

"What sort of problems?" Phil asked.

"A whole range of things," Dad answered. "It turns out Mr. Huehne has quite a drinking problem. When he drinks, he usually will do things like hitting his wife or the kids. One of the reasons Beulah is so tough is that she stands up to her father and protects her mother and the other kids. Apparently a lot of times she ends up getting hit.

"Mrs. Huehne is totally frightened of her husband when he has been drinking. They don't have a lot of money to begin with and Mr. Huehne's drinking uses up a lot of his income.

"As we found out more and more information, we decided what steps had to be taken. The children were our biggest concern. We knew we had to do something because we felt it was only a matter of time before they would get into trouble."

"I think they've already gotten into a lot of trouble," I said.

"I don't think we should be too judgmental," Dad told me. "They have had a tough life."

"Well, what happens now" Mother asked. Apparently Dad had not told her any of the details.

"Leo said he would sit down with Mr. Huehne and explain to him that he was in serious trouble, that Leo would give him a choice: stop drinking, start attending Alcoholics Anonymous meetings, or Leo would get a warrant for his arrest, and he would likely end up in jail."

"Wow," Phil said. "That sounds pretty tough."

"It is, but you and I have never seen Leo's tough side. Remember, he's been with the sheriff's department for a lot of years. He's an experienced police officer," Dad answered.

Dad continued, "Leo did meet with Mr. Huehne. Mr. Huehne didn't want to talk with him until Leo threatened to arrest him and take him to the county jail. Then he got more cooperative. He agreed to try Alcoholics Anonymous and Leo said he would arrange for a member to take Mr. Huehne to the meetings in Ripon. And Leo told him that if he heard he wasn't attending the meetings, he would be in serious trouble."

"Now," Dad went on, "there are still some other issues. The family is in bad shape financially. I'm sure you kids have noticed that the Huehne children don't have very good clothes."

"It must be especially tough for the girl. What's her name?" Mother asked.

"It's Beulah," Phil answered. "I've noticed her clothes aren't very nice."

"The Ladies Aid has that special fund to help people in need," Mother said. "They don't use it much at all, and the money just sits there."

"Why don't you talk with the president of the Aid and see what she thinks?" Dad to said Mother. "Maybe the Aid would be willing to make a donation to buy her some new clothes."

"I'll talk with Mrs. Jungman. I'll be glad to take Beulah clothes shopping," Mother replied.

"Now if we can just figure out how to help them with their finances," Dad answered.

Things worked well. Dad heard from Mr. Rolfs that Mr. Huehne was going to AA meetings. Mother had talked with Mrs. Jungman about what the Ladies Aid could do. It turned out that the the president had the authority to authorize a gift from the fund.

"The Aid apparently approved that years ago so that Aid members wouldn't start gossiping about who was being helped," Mother said.

Dad talked with Mr. Rolfs who arranged to have Beulah excused from school. Mother and Mrs. Jungman took her to Fond du Lac where they went shopping at the Hills Department Store.

At supper that night, Mother went into great detail about the clothes they had bought.

"She got some of the cutest outfits. Does she ever look nice. And while we were there, Mrs. Jungman suggested that Beulah should get her hair done at the HIlls Beauty Salon. She even said she would pay for it. So we did that too. I don't think Beulah really knew what to say. She asked who was doing this and Mrs. Jungman told her that the Ladies Aid of the church had a special fund for things like that. Beulah was just amazed."

The next night at supper Phil reported that Beulah was in school with her new clothes and new hair do.

"You should have seen all the boys looking at her. You would have thought there was a new girl in school or something," he said.

Mother smiled at Phil's comments.

"Now if we could just do something to help the family with their finances," Dad sighed.

The days went by. I noticed that the Huehne kids were rarely a topic of discussion at our supper table.

Except one night.

We were just starting supper when I said, "I think I have an idea for the Huehnes."

"What do you mean?" Phil asked.

"You know, Dad keeps mentioning that he is concerned about their finances. Well, I heard something today that might help," I answered.

Dad put down his fork and looked at me.

"What would that be?" he asked.

"Well, when I was at the locker plant today, getting some vegetables for supper, I heard Mr. Brueggeman saying to Mrs. Brueggeman that he sure wished they could get some extra help at the locker plant. I knew it wasn't any of my business, but I asked what kind of help they were looking for. Mr. Brueggemann said he needed someone to help in the cutting area, wrapping meat and things like that. I thought maybe this is a job Mrs. Huehne could do," I said.

Dad looked thoughtful.

"I think I'll stop and talk with Mr. Brueggemann and explain things. Mr. Brueggemann is a good church man and that should help."

It worked out well. Mrs. Huehne got the job and turned out to be a good worker. Mr. Brueggemann thanked Dad for suggesting her. It looked like that was the end of the story.

It turned out it wasn't.

One night we were just finishing supper when the phone rang. Dad went and answered. We could hear him as we sat at the supper table.

"Yes, I will be home. Yes, I'm certain Mrs. Kurtz would do that. About seven will be fine. Just use the study door—that's the door on the right as you face the house."

What Happened to the Huehne Kids • 133

We heard him hang up the phone, and then he returned to the table. We all waited for him to say something.

"Well, I never know what to expect when the phone rings. That was Beulah Huehne. She wants to come and see me this evening and she asked you to be there too," he said, looking at Mother.

We kids were really curious, but we kept out of sight. Beulah didn't stay long, and after we heard her leave, we all came to the living room, hoping that Dad and Mother would tell us why Beulah had been there.

Dad and Mother came out of the study. Both were smiling.

"What was that all about?" we all asked.

"Beulah said she just couldn't get over the fact that the church cared enough to provide the new clothes for her. She said it really changed her life. She decided that she wants to be confirmed and become a church member. She asked if she would have to go through two years of confirmation class," Dad said.

"What did you tell her? Phil asked.

"I told her that I thought she was an adult and that she could join the adult instruction class which I'll be starting next month. She seemed relieved to know that," Dad said.

"Why did she want Mother there?" I asked.

"I think it's because I got to know her when we went shopping," Mother explained. "She was just more comfortable with me being there."

We kids started to leave.

"Oh," said Dad, "a couple of other things. She said she was going to see that Bub would start confirmation class and that Guerdon would start Sunday School. And she also added that we'd better believe that they'll be there."

Mother smiled. "This certainly has turned out wonderfully well."

She thought for a moment.

"You know, it's just too bad this didn't happen earlier. Then maybe we never would have had that terrible incident at the Rakows."

The rest of us smiled, remembering the time it was hardly a silent night.

RING THE BELL AND COUNT THE PEOPLE

"Well," said Dad after we had said our table prayer and began eating supper, "I have some news."

We paused with our meal. Dad rarely made announcements of this type. He would usually mention things in an offhand manner or more likely, one of us kids would bring it up.

"Did you get a call?" Phil asked.

Pastors' families were always anxious that the pastor might receive a call to a new parish. I knew that Dad had not received a call, at least I was pretty certain he hadn't received one. I picked up the mail from the post office every day, and I would have seen an envelope from the district president's office. Most of the letters Dad got from the office were machine addressed and contained routine district announcements. If an envelope came from the district office that was individually addressed and was a fairly thick envelope, one could figure out it was probably a call. No such envelope had arrived lately, so I was pretty sure that Dad was not going to tell us he had received a call.

"No," replied Dad, "no call."

We all breathed a sigh of relief. No one wanted to move. We liked living in the Village. Being a pastor's family we knew that some day we would probably move, but for now we were happy to stay.

"So what is the news?" my sister demanded. She did not like secrets, especially when she felt she should know things before anyone else.

"Ornie is resigning," Dad told us.

This was NEWS. Ornie had been church janitor for a long time, longer than we had lived in the Village.

"How come he's resigning?" we wanted to know.

"He told me this afternoon and said I should tell the church council at its meeting tonight," Dad explained. The church council was the congregation's board which handled the various business aspects of the church. "Ornie said he has been doing it for all these years, and he feels it's time to step down."

"I didn't think the church janitor's job is all that difficult," I said. " He has to clean the church each week, mow the lawn in the summer and shovel the sidewalk in the winter."

"And he has to ring the bell for services and count the people too," Phil added.

"I think he is just a little tired of having to be at every service every week," Dad guessed. "He certainly doesn't get a big salary either."

"I wonder who will take the job," Mother said. "You know..."

She was interrupted by sobs from my sister.

"What in the world are you crying about?" Mother asked.

Helene brushed away her tears.

"That means I won't get gum any more."

The rest of us laughed. Helene was indignant. This was not a laughing matter.

Each Sunday morning Ornie would stop by the parsonage and pick up the bulletins for the service. Helene would always hand them to him, and he in turn would give her a pack of gum. Since we kids rarely had money of our own to buy such things, the loss of her weekly package of gum was a serious matter for her.

"That's all right," Mother responded. "Maybe it's just as well. Chewing gum really isn't good for your teeth."

This did not satisfy Helene at all. But she brightened up.

"Maybe the new janitor will do like Ornie did," she decided.

We continued to eat supper and the conversation turned to other topics.

Several weeks later Dad mentioned that no one had applied for the janitor's job.

"Ornie talked with me yesterday and said he would sure like it if the church found a new janitor," Dad reported. "I suppose we could run an ad in the Village newspaper to see if there is anyone in town who would take the job. It would be nice if a member of the church would take the job."

No applications were forthcoming. The janitorial position remained unfilled.

One night at supper when we were discussing the situation, I startled the family with a suggestion.

"Why doesn't our family take the job?" I asked. "We're at the church all the time anyway. I mow the lawn at the house here and shovel the walks. It wouldn't be all that hard to do the church as well. Any time there are services or meetings, Dad is always there, so he could open the church and turn on the lights, just like Ornie does."

Dad seemed interested.

"It doesn't pay a whole lot, but the extra income would help," Dad noted.

"We would need to do the weekly cleaning and we could all help with that," I continued.

"What about ringing the bell and counting the people?" Helene wanted to know.

"Well," I answered. I think I could do it."

"That's a pretty big bell. It even lifts Ornie off his feet when he stops the ringing," Phil pointed out.

That was true. It was a big bell. One thing you didn't want to do was to have the bell stop ringing with a weak clang or two. No, the bell had to be brought to a stop, so the last ring would be a firm sound.

"I can give it a try. Ornie will show me how to do it," I said.

We talked it over some more and decided it would be worth trying.

"The council meets tonight. If there are no applications, I'll mention it and see what the councilmen think. If no one objects, they'll probably go along with the idea," Dad said.

The next day Dad reported that the council had approved hiring our family as the church janitors.

"They seemed glad that we were willing to take the job," he commented.

"They probably figured that now they won't have to give you a raise this year," Mother countered.

Ring the Bell and Count the People • 137

Helene sighed, "I suppose that means no more gum on Sunday mornings."

We exchanged glances and decided it was probably not the time to comment about oral hygiene.

Ornie showed us how things were done.

"Come to the church on Sunday when I ring the early bell, and I'll show you how it's done and let you try it," he told me.

The church bell was rung at 8:30, a half hour before Sunday School started. It would then be rung again at 9 to mark the start of Sunday School and then at 10:30 at the start of services.

The next Sunday I climbed the balcony steps a little before 8:30. Ornie was there waiting for me. He looked at his watch.

"Two minutes," he said. He showed me the two ropes.

"The heavy rope is for ringing the bell. The lighter rope is when you toll the bell for funerals and when you ring it for deaths," he explained.

I had forgotten about funerals. The church had the custom that when a member died, the janitor would go to the church, ring the bell for a few peals and then slowly toll the bell, one stroke for each year of the person's age. When this happened, the telephone in the parsonage started ringing with the question,

"Who died?" or "Did Mrs. Ruenglin die?"

"You have to count carefully when you're tolling the bell," Ornie told me. "Everybody in town counts, and you better get the age right, otherwise you'll hear about it. I remember when Mrs. Loefler died. She was 102. I was certain I had counted right, but three people told me I had tolled the bell 103 times."

Ornie looked at his watch and said, "OK, you grasp the rope high and give it a good pull to get it started."

He proceeded to pull the rope, and the big bell began pealing out its sound.

He rang it a few times and then motioned for me to take the rope.

"Keep pulling it even," he told me. "I usually ring it about 40 times.

I continued to pull the rope.

"OK, now, to stop it, you need to quit pulling the rope and then hold it tight. You want to have the bell sound strong until the end, not kind of dribble off," Ornie said. "Now, stop ringing and hold on."

I did as instructed and was immediately pulled about three feet off the floor, But the bell stopped on a strong note.

Ornie chuckled.

"It lifts me off the floor too; although not that high. You've got the idea about how it works."

So our family took over the janitorial duties. I found I was doing most of the work: cleaning the sanctuary and basement every week; mowing the lawn in summer and shoveling in winter, ringing the bell and counting the people in attendance at services.

One evening in fall, the phone rang. Dad answered it.

"I"m sorry to hear that. I'll be over in a few minutes. By the way, how old was she?" I heard him say.

Dad hung up the phone.

"Mrs. Stoffhager died. I'm going over to the house to have a prayer with the family."

Dad looked at me. "You'll have to go to church to toll the bell. Remember, you ring it first for about one minute and then toll it. She was 79. Let me write it down so you won't forget."

I went to the church, turned on the balcony light and climbed the steps. The rest of the church was totally dark.

I grabbed the bell rope, gave it a good pull and the sound of the big bell broke the quiet of the Village evening. After five or six pulls, I grabbed the rope, got lifted off the floor. I then reached for the smaller rope.

The bell was rung by pulling the rope around the wheel which swung the bell back and forth. In tolling the bell, the rope which was tied to a large hammer hit the inside of the bell.

I began tolling the bell.

One, two, three...

I slowly counted the strokes.

Don't miscount, I told myself.

43, 44, 45...

I kept tolling.

Finally, 79 and I stopped. .

Ring the Bell and Count the People • 139

I climbed down the stairs, turned off the lights and walked next door to the parsonage.

"Good job," Mother told me. "I counted 79, just as it was supposed to be."

The next day Dad told me that the funeral would be in three days, and I would have to get excused from school in the afternoon to toll the bell for the funeral.

"I'll write a note to Mr. Franklin." he added.

I was further surprised the day after the funeral. When I came home from school, Dad handed me an envelope.

"What's this?" I asked.

"Fred Forest, the funeral director, stopped by with it for you."

I opened the envelope. Inside was a five dollar bill with a statement which said "Janitor expenses for funeral."

Hey, being church janitor isn't all that bad, I thought. Five dollars, why Phil only makes ten dollars a week at his job at the gas station.

I immediately began mentally evaluating the physical condition of our older members. Not that I wished any harm to them, but.. . .

"May I keep this? I asked Dad.

"Yes," Dad assured me. "I would not mention it to kids in your class, however."

I nodded.

Several weeks later at supper Dad started talking about the church council meeting that evening.

"I'm going to finally tell the council that it's time to discontinue the German Christmas Day service," he announced.

"Do you think they'll agree?" Mother wondered.

Emanuel had been founded by German immigrants. Up until World War I, all services had been in German. English services were gradually introduced. When Dad first came to Emanuel, there were German services every other Sunday. Slowly the number of German services was reduced, and for the past several years, the only remaining German service was on Christmas Day. We kids liked it since that meant we didn't have to attend the service We figured that we had gone twice on Christmas Eve and that was enough.

"Well," Dad rejoined, "last year we had five people there plus the organist, janitor and preacher. Since then, Mrs. Stoffhager and Mr. Heinzmeier have died. August Stolzman is bedridden, so that leaves only Mrs. Ausmann, and she's so deaf, there would be no use preaching a sermon. and oh, yes, Rolland Berwald who only comes because he likes to sing 'Oh, du Froeliche.'"

"I sure hope the council sees the point," Mother said.

Now there was something I hadn't thought of. If there was a German service, I would have to go and ring the bell. Counting the attendance was not a problem. If there was no German service, there would be a regular service, and I would also have to go.

The next day Dad reported that the council had approved dropping the service.

"A couple of the councilmen said we may as well not have any service on Christmas Day since everyone had gotten out of the habit of going to Christmas Day services. I need to come up with a plan to assure a good attendance."

A couple of nights later at dinner, Dad started talking right after we said the table prayer.

"I think I know what we can do for Christmas Day," he began. "I am going to ask Gordy to give the sermon."

Gordy was a member of the congregation who was studying for the ministry.

"Last Easter he preached at the sunrise service, and people really thought he did a good job. I think they would like to hear him preach again. Phil, would you be willing to do the liturgy?"

Dad had been encouraging Phil to take an occasional role in the service, hoping that he might begin considering the ministry.

"Oh," Phil hesitated a bit, "I guess I could."

"Then we'll have the junior choir and senior choir sing. That means all of their families will come, so we should have a pretty good attendance." Dad smiled at the thought.

So it was decided. No more German Christmas Day service. There would be a Christmas Day service with special music and a guest preacher.

"And," Dad announced, "this means I can sit with the family which will be a special treat for me."

"Ah, just a minute, Dad," interjected Phil. "Since I have to do the liturgy, I will be sitting up in front by the altar."

"And I'll be singing in the junior choir," Helene pointed out.

"And I'll be singing with the senior choir," Mother added.

Dad looked at me.

"Well, Dad, if you want to sit up in the balcony with me while I ring the bell and count the people, I'll be glad to have company," I answered.

So Christmas Day came. The service went well, Gordy had a good sermon. The choirs sang. The attendance was much better than the council had expected.

And no one noticed that Dad was sitting in the front pew by himself.

THE YEAR COMES TO AN END

It was New Year's Eve. We were sitting at the supper table. There were just four of us. Phil wasn't there. He and Margie were going out for supper and to a movie.

"Well," said Mother as we were eating, "this is what it will be like when Phil goes away to college. There will just be the four of us at meal time."

"When will that be?" Helene wanted to know.

"It won't be until next year," Mother replied, looking a little sad.

This hadn't occurred to me before. I knew Phil would be going to college after he graduated from high school. Mother was always talking about when we kids would go to college. We were constantly encouraged to save our money, so we would have a bank account when we were ready to go

But college seemed like such a long ways away. And now Mother was talking about when Phil would be gone. I realized why Mother looked sad. But I thought, this was no time to be sad. It was New Year's Eve—the end of a great year, and the start of a brand new one.

For many people, New Year's Eve was a big party night. For the parsonage family, it was a quiet evening. We used to have a church service. Dad called it Sylvester Eve. I remember asking him one time who Sylvester was, and Dad had to admit he didn't know for certain.

"I guess he might have been an old-time saint. It's just that New Year's Eve has always been called 'Sylvester Eve,'" Dad answered.

The Year Comes to an End • 143

However, several years ago, the church council had decided to cancel the service since it was getting so hardly anyone came any more.

"People would rather go out and party," Mother complained. We kids didn't mind. We figured we had gone to enough church services during the holiday season, especially now that there was a service on Christmas Day.

Although we just were planning to spend a quiet evening at home, there was one event to be observed. At midnight I would go the church and ring the bell. It was a custom in the Village that the churches would ring their bells at midnight to welcome the New Year. Since Emanuel had the biggest bell, it led off the bell ringing. The other church bells would then join in: the Evangelical United Brethren, the Methodist, Bethel Reformed and St. Brendan's Catholic.

"Can I stay up until midnight to hear the bells ring?" Helene asked.

"That's pretty late for you," Mother replied. "Let's see if you stay awake until then."

To pass the time after supper, the four of us played Rook. Rook is a Parker Brothers card game. Mother approved of our playing it since it did not use regular playing cards. Instead of having clubs, diamonds, hearts and spades, it had colors: black, green, red and yellow. Mother had grown up in a branch of Norwegian Lutheranism which frowned on card playing, so from her viewpoint it was OK to play Rook since it did not use sinful playing cards. When I asked her why playing cards were sinful, Mother was never able gave a good answer.

"Dad plays solitaire," I once pointed out.

"Well, that's different," Mother answered. She did not go into detail on why it was different, so I decided to drop the subject.

"It has certainly been a good year," Dad reminisced as he shuffled the cards. "What did you like best?"

"I liked going to the state fair and being in the parade and having the governor show me how to eat a cream puff and winning the prize for singing at the centennial celebration. and. . ." Helene paused for breath, trying to think of what else she had done.

"Yes, " Mother agreed, "it has been quite a year for us. And I'm glad that our Christmas this year was nice and peaceful, not like last year."

The rest of us smiled, remembering everything which had happened a year ago at Christmas time.

Mother was right, I thought, Christmas was a lot quieter this year compared with a year ago.

We talked more about the past year. About the Sunday School picnic, the time when the station was burglarized, about Cousin George's stay with us and when the pigs escaped from Uncle Alfred's farm and all the other things which happened last year.

We all agreed—it had been quite a year.

"What do you suppose the New Year will be like?" Helene wondered.

"We'll just have to wait and see, won't we?" said Dad as he dealt the last card and picked up his hand.

APPRECIATION

Penny Moniz, the Language Arts teacher at the Brandon, Wisconsin, Middle School, tells her students that books don't magically appear on the shelves of Barnes and Noble—authors have to write them. She's right, of course. (Teachers usually are.) And a writer just doesn't magically produce a book.

This book, like most books, became a reality because a lot of people helped me in one way or another. I am indebted to many people. Here is my thank you to them.

Thank you to the readers who said nice things about *Hardly a Silent Night* and encouraged me to write a sequel. Their enthusiasm is what motivated me to write this book.

Also, I thank the many people who provided me with information, ideas and help in recounting what life was like when the stories in this book took place. And there were others who helped me in various ways. If I were more organized I would have carefully noted each person's contribution, but since I am not organized, I'll have to rely on my memory. So a big note of thanks goes to Richard Damerau, Galen Burke, Bob Westphal, Dave Johnson, Mike Miller, Penny Moniz, Don Marschall and Helene Kurtz Stadtmueller.

I owe special thanks to the great folks in Brandon who helped in one way or another: Twilah Meenk DeBoer, Karey Bremer Schmidt, Tylor Loest, Carolyn Dahlke and Nancy Paul, I have to add a warm word of thanks to Sharon Krohn and Charleen Strook of the Everlasting Garden Scents gift store in Brandon for their interest and support. I can't tell you how much I have enjoyed meeting with the students at the Brandon School. They are a great bunch of kids, taught by a outstanding staff of educators.

I would be remiss if I did not pay tribute to my teachers at Brandon. To Esther Zacho who taught me how to read. To Agnes

Loomans Koehler who always encouraged me to read once I had my assignments completed. To Genevieve Dobbyns who tolerated my laughter while I was supposedly reading quietly at my desk. To Bill Fenelon who encouraged students to read by giving every student a book at Christmas time.

To fellow members at St. Philip's Lutheran Church and friends at Lyngblomsten who told me they enjoyed my book. Thank you so much.

To family and friends who listened as I read drafts of chapters. Not only did you stay awake, but you laughed at the right places—mostly.

I am indebted to my family for their help and encouragement. To son, Steve, for his technical assistance on the computer, to son Dave for his continued interest, to daughter in law Beth and grandchildren Emily and Joshua who like my stories.

A special thanks to Leonard Flachman and Karen Walhof at Kirk House Publishers for their work in turning the manuscript into the book you are reading.

Finally, my appreciation to the editor-in-chief, my wife Grace. How fortunate I am to have such a skilled and patient helpmate who overlooks the fact that I have never quite learned the proper use of the comma and gently makes needed improvements and corrections. Thank you, Grace. This book, as well as the others, never would have seen the light of day without you.

Harold Kurtz

ABOUT THE AUTHOR

Harold Kurtz was born in Milwaukee, but spent most of his early life in Brandon, Wisconsin, a village of 708 people in western Fond du Lac County. His father was the pastor of Emanuel Lutheran Church in Brandon. Harold lived in the parsonage with his family: Mother, Father, his older brother Philip and younger sister Helene.

He began his education at Carlton School in Milwaukee and continued his education in the Brandon schools. The family moved from Brandon during Harold's sophomore year in high school. He went on to graduate from high school in Platteville, Wisconsin.

He earned his bachelor's degree at Wartburg College in Waverly, Iowa, and a master's degree in journalism from the University of Wisconsin in Madison. After a short career as a journalist with the Appleton, Wisconsin, *Post-Crescent,* he went into institutional advancement work, holding positions in Park Ridge, Illinois; Milwaukee and St. Paul-Minneapolis.

He is the author of six other published books including *Hardly a Silent Night,* published in 2004.

He and his wife Grace live in New Brighton, Minnesota.